Relationship Vision

Couples Reconnection Journal

Daily Conversations, Relationship Questions and Bucket Lists to Fix Your Marriage & Be Happy

Conversations to manifest an intentional life together

3 Years. 365 Questions. 1095 Conversations to manifest an intentional life together.

Rabbi Shlomo Slatkin, M.S., LCPC
with Rivka Slatkin,
Relationship Experts and Presenters
of the Getting the Love You Want Worldwide Workshop

ISBN 978-1-70641-993-8 (paperback)

Copyright © 2020 by Shlomo Slatkin

All rights reserved. No part of this publication may be reproduced, distributed, or transmitted in any form or by any means, including photocopying, recording, or other electronic or mechanical methods without the prior written permission of the publisher. For permission requests, solicit the publisher via the address below.

Independently Published

Printed in the United States of America

Preface

As a marriage counselor in practice for over a decade, I've seen all sorts of couples ranging from those wanting to make a good marriage great to couples in extreme crisis. Hundreds of couples have gone through our 2 Day "No Blame, No Shame" Marriage Restoration Retreat as well as the worldwide Getting the Love You Want Workshop created by Dr. Harville Hendrix, founder of Imago Relationship Therapy, that my wife Rivka and I present together.

Our retreat and workshop format involves two days of intensive exploration of both yourself and your spouse- why you fell in love, why things may have gotten more difficult over time, and a clear path for how to bring back love and affection as well as tools for moving forward in life together, happily.

Sometimes couples find that focusing on their issues and frustrations with each other helps them get to the root of their problems and once they discover safe ways to connect and communicate, this does the "trick" for them. Other couples respond better to a consistent infusion of positive and fun activities without a focus on the more troubling issues.

At our intensive retreats we offer both paths for optimal success.

This beautiful journal, The Relationship Vision Couples Reconnection Journal is designed for you to infuse positivity and fun into your relationship, thereby also working on some of the harder aspects of your marriage, without it seeming a chore.

You'll go through questions and conversation prompts, one after the next - some a continuation of the question before it - with varying levels of intensity to correspond to whatever mood you and your partner are in that day. If your relationship has been struggling, start with the easier questions. If you're ready to deepen things and work on some things that you've been getting stuck on, try the harder section.

As a marriage counselor with the interest of keeping couples together and happy, you will never have to worry about questions in this journal making things worse for you both as some other journals do in their line of questioning. Stick to our instructions and guidelines for both asking and answering the questions in a way that fosters emotional safety and connection with your partner, a goal that we are excited to help you achieve through this reconnection journal!

With best wishes for your relationship success,
Rabbi Shlomo and Rivka Slatkin
TheMarriageRestorationProject.com

Introduction

Life is busy. So busy. And it's easy to get lost in the day to day responsibilities and forget each other. The Relationship Vision Couples Reconnection Journal is designed for you to remember each other, why you fell in love, when, where, and how, so that you can cocreate and design the next years of your life together; craft a joint mission statement that you actually fulfill, and keep the romance and deep connection alive.

Because we believe you fell in love for a reason. That reason is why you picked each other above everyone else you ever dated.

Spending time to learn more about yourselves, your partner, learning more about what is meaningful to you and then culling those conversations into a joint "couples mission statement" for your future life together is going to keep you on the path of happiness and deep connection.

What could be better than that?

Chapter One

Daily Conversation and Relationship Questions

We start with daily questions for you to answer, ideally, WITH each other as a way to connect everyday.

Some of these questions are easy and some are harder.

Harder because you may feel reactive upon hearing your spouse's answer and you want to retort back.

Harder because the question is asking you to be vulnerable with your partner.

The good news is that we've separated these relationship questions into three different sections; easy, medium, hard.

The easy questions may seem silly at times but know that they're doing exactly what they're supposed to be doing. Giving you things to laugh and smile about with your partner, helping to bring about warm and fuzzy feelings that are oh so important in building a life together. Don't discount these questions!

Please don't judge yourself or your partner if you choose to stay in the easy "lane" of questioning. It's simply where you are at now and within your comfort zone.

The hope is that as you learn how to talk and listen, both you and your partner will feel safer to express yourself and share as time goes on.

A few ground rules for sharing and listening (***which is much harder for some!***). Listening is other focused. This means, not responding, reacting, offering advice, or even commiserating. The safest thing you can do is just be quiet and say nothing. A more active way of listening is called mirroring. This means reflecting back, like a mirror, what your partner shares with you verbatim. This is helpful for many reasons. We tend to interpret external stimuli through our own lens. What often happens is that we misinterpret, leading to miscommunication and often conflict. By mirroring, you are focused on exactly what the other said, not your spin on it and you make sure you got it right. After repeating back, you can check and see, "did I get you?" If not, let your partner repeat. Once you got it, ask "is there more?" giving a safe opportunity to continue opening up.

Another reason to mirror is that much of the time, all we really want is to feel heard. We don't want a response or a rebuttal. Mirroring alone can help us deescalate and feel better. Finally, it helps the listener stay other focused. Instead of responding or getting reactive, the listener's sole job is to reflect back. This helps the listener not take it personally, and stay calm. When you listen to partner's responses in this way, you can prevent a potentially touchy topic from exploding into major conflict.

Another way to keep the sharing safe is to schedule a time to do this work. Make sure your partner is available to listen. Otherwise, if you catch him/her off guard, it is a sure way to set your self up for the opposite of what you want. When you do share, make sure you use "I" statements. Focus on yourself and your feelings as opposed to what your spouse does or does not do. This way you make your sharing safer and less likely to provoke your partner. Finally, make sure your language is not laced with negativity or sarcasm. This only seeks to pollute the space when your goal is to develop a deeper connection. If you follow these guidelines, you are more likely to achieve the intended goal of these exercises.

We've included questions that are going to give you the opportunity to talk about funny, embarrassing, financial, spiritual, future, critical, and things from your past. All are important as they serve as a way for you to deeply get to know your spouse, see them as the child that they once were, knowing that despite you being married and committed to each other, your spouse is actually a unique world of his/her own, with different experiences, viewpoints, mindsets, and passions.

Your job is to be as a guest, traveling across the bridge into another "land". A land where you may not- at first glance -understand the language or want to adopt their customs, but as a traveler, it is not your job to judge whether or not their language sounds good or their traditions acceptable. You are simply a tourist.

You'll want to be the best guest that has ever visited this land, so that one day you will be "invited back". Being invited back willingly looks like your spouse enjoying sharing with you and wanting to tell you more, feeling more and more comfortable with you in their world, because you aren't a loud or obnoxious guest- complaining about the food or not understanding the language in this place- but a gentle, respectful observer in this new strange land.

That is how emotional safety and connection is built. No blame and no shame.

Feel free to start with one question a day or a few questions at a time should you have some blissful uninterrupted time together.

If you're listening on audio, simply pause the recording when you wish to pause your work for the day.

After you've completed the questions over some time, you will know much more about your partner and be able to progress into the next step of this book which is to list caring behaviors that you now know your spouse wishes that you would do, romantic gestures your spouse would love, as well as fun, future high energy adventures that you both wish to cross off your bucket list to do together.

The final goal of this book is for you to be able to draft a complete joint relationship vision together.

What is a relationship vision?

Think of it as a joint mission statement.

🔊 mis·sion state·ment

noun

a formal summary of the aims and values of a company, organization, or individual.
"a mission statement to which all employees can subscribe"

Just like in a business, the company needs a formal statement so all employees know the goal of the organization and where they are headed, having a vision provides us direction to reach our destination and helps us focus our energy to get there.

Without it, we may feel aimless, chaotic, and empty. This is especially true with marriage. A lot of couples get married and assume the relationship will take care of itself. Sooner or later they realize that it is not so easy. They both entered the marriage with their own unconscious ideas of how their relationship would be, with separate desires, dreams, values, and needs. Many early frustrations in a marriage arise when husband and wife butt heads about these very issues, discovering that they are not on the same page.

Whether or not you have already woken up to the reality that some degree of conflict is inevitable in relationships, it is essential for you to co-create a conscious shared vision. How do you want to build your home? What are its foundations? The following exercise, based on the work of Dr. Harville Hendrix, author of *Getting the Love You Want,* is an effective tool to help couples create this vision.

Are you ready to begin?

We're going to get you started on your journey towards crafting your relationship vision through answering easy, medium, and harder relationship questions.

Why do we start with conversations for you to have and questions for you to ask before working on your joint mission statement?

Because we want to give you the opportunity to get to know each other even more deeply than you thought possible. You'll learn new things about your spouse that you didn't even know was important to them! It's those golden discoveries that will help you create an even more beautiful future vision for your life together.

You can flip back and forth between the easy, medium, and harder questions if you choose or work slowly through one section at a time.

If your relationship is not in the best place right now, you'll want to stick to the easy and medium section of questioning, until the questions help you get to a better place through the fun and healthier interactions that you'll start having with each other by virtue of spending some time daily to reconnect with each other.

That's why we call this audio book the "Couples Reconnection Journal".

Feel free to be as flexible with the completion of the questions. You can decide to answer one question a day- say, before you go to bed each night- or once a week on a preplanned date night, whatever you decide, make sure that you've created an "appointment" with your spouse to ask him/her these relationship questions though. That's because we want you to work on the habit of always making sure it's a good time to talk.

You can skip ahead, answer the questions completely out of order- all of the questions are for you to take your time answering- preferably together- whenever convenient for the both of you.

We've got enough questions and conversation starters to last you over two years so you'll have plenty to talk about.

Section One

Relationship Questions
Easiest level of intensity

1. *What does the ideal life look like?*
   You: _____
   _____
   _____

   Your spouse: _____
   _____
   _____

2. *What does it mean to die well?*
   You: _____
   _____
   _____

   Your spouse: _____
   _____
   _____

3. *Who do you know who is living life to the fullest?*
   You: _____
   _____
   _____

   Your spouse: _____
   _____
   _____

4. *If you died today what regrets would you have about your life?*
   You: _____
   _____
   _____
   _____

   Your spouse: _____
   _____
   _____
   _____

5. *Who had the biggest impact on you growing up?*
   You: _____
   _____
   _____
   _____

   Your spouse: _____
   _____
   _____
   _____

6. *What are your hobbies?*
   You: _____
   _____
   _____
   _____

   Your spouse: _____
   _____
   _____
   _____

7. *If you could have dinner with any 3 people, dead or alive, who would they be and why?*
   You: _____
   _____
   _____
   _____

   Your spouse: _____
   _____
   _____
   _____

8. *What sorts of things make you laugh?*
   You: _____
   _____
   _____
   _____

   Your spouse: _____
   _____
   _____
   _____

9. *What is your biggest goal?*
   You: _____
   _____
   _____
   _____

   Your spouse: _____
   _____
   _____
   _____

10. What are your pet peeves?
    You: _____
    _____
    _____
    _____

    Your spouse: _____
    _____
    _____
    _____

11. What do you like to do on the weekend?
    You: _____
    _____
    _____
    _____

    Your spouse: _____
    _____
    _____
    _____

12. What is the story behind any nicknames you had?
    You: _____
    _____
    _____
    _____

    Your spouse: _____
    _____
    _____
    _____

13. *What was your favorite tv show growing up?*
    You: _____
    _____
    _____
    _____

    Your spouse: _____
    _____
    _____
    _____

14. *What are your favorite shows now?*
    You: _____
    _____
    _____
    _____

    Your spouse: _____
    _____
    _____
    _____

15. *What are your favorite movies?*
    You: _____
    _____
    _____

    Your spouse: _____
    _____
    _____

16. *Tell me one thing that would surprise me about you?*
    You: _____
    _____
    _____
    _____

    Your spouse: _____
    _____
    _____
    _____

17. *What attracts you most in a girl?*
    You: _____
    _____
    _____
    _____

    Your spouse: _____
    _____
    _____
    _____

18. *What attracts you most in a guy?*
    You: _____
    _____
    _____
    _____

    Your spouse: _____
    _____
    _____
    _____

19. *What were you like as a kid?*
    You: _____
    _____
    _____

    Your spouse: _____
    _____
    _____

20. *What are some things on your bucket list?*
    You: _____
    _____
    _____

    Your spouse: _____
    _____
    _____

21. *Have you found your calling, if so what is it?*
    You: _____
    _____
    _____

    Your spouse: _____
    _____
    _____

22. *Who has been the biggest influence in your life?*
You: _____
_____
_____
_____

Your spouse: _____
_____
_____
_____

23. *Name all the pets you've had?*
You: _____
_____
_____
_____

Your spouse: _____
_____
_____
_____

24. *What's a challenge in life that you had to overcome and how did you overcome it?*
You: _____
_____
_____
_____

Your spouse: _____
_____
_____
_____

25. *If you could only listen to one song for the rest of your life, what would it be and why?*
    You: _____
    _____
    _____

    Your spouse: _____
    _____
    _____

26. *If you could only watch one movie for the rest of your life, what would it be and why?*
    You: _____
    _____
    _____

    Your spouse: _____
    _____
    _____

27. *If you could only eat one food for the rest of your life, what would it be and why?*
    You: _____
    _____
    _____

    Your spouse: _____
    _____
    _____

28. What is your favorite childhood memory and what made it so special to you?

You: _____

_____

_____

Your spouse: _____

_____

_____

29. What is your favorite commercial that you've ever seen and why?

You: _____

_____

_____

Your spouse: _____

_____

_____

30. If you could give your younger self one piece of advice what would it be?

You: _____

_____

_____

Your spouse: _____

_____

_____

31. If you were stuck on a deserted island and you could only bring one thing what would it be and why?
    You: _____
    _____
    _____

    Your spouse: _____
    _____
    _____

32. Who is your celebrity crush?
    You: _____
    _____
    _____

    Your spouse: _____
    _____
    _____

33. Who is your favorite music artist?
    You: _____
    _____
    _____

    Your spouse: _____
    _____
    _____

34. *What is your favorite music genre?*
    You: _____
    _____
    _____
    _____

    Your spouse: _____
    _____
    _____
    _____

35. *What is your favorite broadway musical?*
    You: _____
    _____
    _____
    _____

    Your spouse: _____
    _____
    _____
    _____

36. *What is your favorite cartoon?*
    You: _____
    _____
    _____
    _____

    Your spouse: _____
    _____
    _____
    _____

37. *What is your favorite music album?*
    You: _____
    _____
    _____

    Your spouse: _____
    _____
    _____

38. *What is your favorite color?*
    You: _____
    _____
    _____

    Your spouse: _____
    _____
    _____

39. *What would you do if you won a million dollars?*
    You: _____
    _____
    _____

    Your spouse: _____
    _____
    _____

40. *If you could have one superpower, what would it be?*
You: _____
_____
_____
_____

Your spouse: _____
_____
_____
_____

41. *What would your superhero name be?*
You: _____
_____
_____
_____

Your spouse: _____
_____
_____
_____

42. *What would be your dream vacation?*
You: _____
_____
_____
_____

Your spouse: _____
_____
_____
_____

43. Which actor/actress could play you in a movie about your life?
    You: _____
    _____
    _____

    Your spouse: _____
    _____
    _____

44. If you could be on any reality tv show what would it be?
    You: _____
    _____
    _____

    Your spouse: _____
    _____
    _____

45. If you could trade lives with anyone for a day, who would it be and why?
    You: _____
    _____
    _____

    Your spouse: _____
    _____
    _____

46. What's your favorite book?
   You: _____
   _____
   _____
   _____

   Your spouse: _____
   _____
   _____
   _____

47. Who is your favorite author?
   You: _____
   _____
   _____
   _____

   Your spouse: _____
   _____
   _____
   _____

48. Which celebrity do you admire most and why?
   You: _____
   _____
   _____
   _____

   Your spouse: _____
   _____
   _____
   _____

49. *What countries have you traveled to?*
    You: _____
    _____
    _____

    Your spouse: _____
    _____
    _____

50. *What is your favorite drink?*
    You: _____
    _____
    _____

    Your spouse: _____
    _____
    _____

51. *If you could move anywhere where would it be?*
    You: _____
    _____
    _____

    Your spouse: _____
    _____
    _____

52. When did you first know you loved me?
    You: _____
    _____
    _____
    _____

    Your spouse: _____
    _____
    _____
    _____

53. What is your favorite part of your body?
    You: _____
    _____
    _____
    _____

    Your spouse: _____
    _____
    _____
    _____

54. What is your favorite part of my body?
    You: _____
    _____
    _____
    _____

    Your spouse: _____
    _____
    _____
    _____

55. *If money was no object what would you do for the rest of your life?*
   You: _____
   _____
   _____

   Your spouse: _____
   _____
   _____

56. *What's 1 thing you've wanted to do with me that we haven't done yet?*
   You: _____
   _____
   _____

   Your spouse: _____
   _____
   _____

57. *If you could have a plane ticket, where would you go?*
   You: _____
   _____
   _____

   Your spouse: _____
   _____
   _____

58. How would you like to spend a night?
You: _____
_____
_____
_____

Your spouse: _____
_____
_____
_____

59. What is the worst pickup line you've ever heard?
You: _____
_____
_____
_____

Your spouse: _____
_____
_____
_____

60. Are you a night owl or a morning person and why?
You: _____
_____
_____
_____

Your spouse: _____
_____
_____
_____

61. *Do you like social media?*
    You: _____
    _____
    _____

    Your spouse: _____
    _____
    _____

62. *What is the craziest thing you've ever done?*
    You: _____
    _____
    _____

    Your spouse: _____
    _____
    _____

63. *What is your favorite city?*
    You: _____
    _____
    _____

    Your spouse: _____
    _____
    _____

64. What is special about the place you grew up?
You: _____
_____
_____
_____

Your spouse: _____
_____
_____
_____

65. What is the worst moment in your life and why?
You: _____
_____
_____
_____

Your spouse: _____
_____
_____
_____

66. What are your favorite date nights and why?
You: _____
_____
_____
_____

Your spouse: _____
_____
_____
_____

67. *What would you wear on a first date and why?*
    You: _____
    _____
    _____

    Your spouse: _____
    _____
    _____

68. *What is your favorite thing to do when you are free?*
    You: _____
    _____
    _____

    Your spouse: _____
    _____
    _____

69. *What are your favorite clothes and why?*
    You: _____
    _____
    _____

    Your spouse: _____
    _____
    _____

70. What was your favorite tradition as a child?
    You: _____
    _____
    _____

    Your spouse: _____
    _____
    _____

71. What was your favorite year in school?
    You: _____
    _____
    _____

    Your spouse: _____
    _____
    _____

72. If you could live during any time in history, when would it be and why?
    You: _____
    _____
    _____

    Your spouse: _____
    _____
    _____

73. What was your favorite family vacation and why?
   You: _____

   Your spouse: _____

74. What was your favorite couple vacation and why?
   You: _____

   Your spouse: _____

75. Who was your favorite teacher in school?
   You: _____

   Your spouse: _____

76. *What is the last text message you sent?*
    You: _____
    _____
    _____
    _____

    Your spouse: _____
    _____
    _____
    _____

77. *What is the last text message you received?*
    You: _____
    _____
    _____
    _____

    Your spouse: _____
    _____
    _____
    _____

78. *What is the last thing you ate?*
    You: _____
    _____
    _____
    _____

    Your spouse: _____
    _____
    _____
    _____

79. *What is the last thing you drank?*
    You: _____
    _____
    _____

    Your spouse: _____
    _____
    _____

80. *What is your favorite ice cream flavor?*
    You: _____
    _____
    _____

    Your spouse: _____
    _____
    _____

81. *Where do you want to be right now?*
    You: _____
    _____
    _____

    Your spouse: _____
    _____
    _____

82. What bands have you seen live?
You: _____
_____
_____
_____

Your spouse: _____
_____
_____
_____

83. What is your idea of a perfect date?
You: _____
_____
_____
_____

Your spouse: _____
_____
_____
_____

84. What movie will you never watch again?
You: _____
_____
_____
_____

Your spouse: _____
_____
_____
_____

85. *What is your favorite time of year and why?*
    You: _____
    _____
    _____

    Your spouse: _____
    _____
    _____

86. *What is your favorite flower?*
    You: _____
    _____
    _____

    Your spouse: _____
    _____
    _____

87. *What was weird about your day?*
    You: _____
    _____
    _____

    Your spouse: _____
    _____
    _____

88. *What word are you using too much lately?*
    You: _____
    _____
    _____

    Your spouse: _____
    _____
    _____

89. *What are three things you need to do tomorrow?*
    You: _____
    _____
    _____

    Your spouse: _____
    _____
    _____

90. *What pictures were on your walls as a teenager?*
    You: _____
    _____
    _____

    Your spouse: _____
    _____
    _____

91. What is the first outfit you remember wearing?
    You: _____
    _____
    _____
    _____

    Your spouse: _____
    _____
    _____
    _____

92. What was your bedroom like as a child?
    You: _____
    _____
    _____
    _____

    Your spouse: _____
    _____
    _____
    _____

93. If you could have witnessed one event in history what would it be?
    You: _____
    _____
    _____
    _____

    Your spouse: _____
    _____
    _____
    _____

94. When you were a child, what did you want to grow up to be?
    You: _____
    _____
    _____
    _____

    Your spouse: _____
    _____
    _____
    _____

95. Where is the most unexpected place you have ever been?
    You: _____
    _____
    _____
    _____

    Your spouse: _____
    _____
    _____
    _____

96. What is something you dream of owning?
    You: _____
    _____
    _____
    _____

    Your spouse: _____
    _____
    _____
    _____

97. What was your favorite toy as a child?
    You: _____

    Your spouse: _____

98. What is the best meal/food I have ever made for you?
    You: _____

    Your spouse: _____

99. If you were going to write a book, what would it be about?
    You: _____

    Your spouse: _____

100. If you could be a genius in one subject, what would it be?
You: _____
_____
_____

Your spouse: _____
_____
_____

101. What is something I do that makes you laugh?
You: _____
_____
_____

Your spouse: _____
_____
_____

102. Would you rather go without internet or showering for a month?
You: _____
_____
_____

Your spouse: _____
_____
_____

103. Would you rather always be overdressed or underdressed?
You: _____

Your spouse: _____

104. Would you rather have your own private island or your own private jet?
You: _____

Your spouse: _____

105. Do you like your name? What would you change it to?
You: _____

Your spouse: _____

106. Do you consider yourself a romantic?
    You: _____

    Your spouse: _____

107. Who do you want to be closer to?
    You: _____

    Your spouse: _____

108. What is the strangest thing you've ever eaten?
    You: _____

    Your spouse: _____

109. *Have you ever met someone famous?*
You: _____

_____

_____

Your spouse: _____

_____

_____

110. *Do you prefer swimming in pools or the ocean?*
You: _____

_____

_____

Your spouse: _____

_____

_____

111. *What would you do if you found $50 on the ground?*
You: _____

_____

_____

Your spouse: _____

_____

_____

112. *If you had to have a tattoo, what would it be and where?*
    You: _____
    _____
    _____

    Your spouse: _____
    _____
    _____

113. *What do you find hilarious that most people don't find funny?*
    You: _____
    _____
    _____

    Your spouse: _____
    _____
    _____

114. *What's your favorite thing to do on the internet?*
    You: _____
    _____
    _____

    Your spouse: _____
    _____
    _____

115. What fad have you held on to even though it's no longer popular?
You: _____
_____
_____
_____

Your spouse: _____
_____
_____
_____

116. What do you spend way too much money on?
You: _____
_____
_____
_____

Your spouse: _____
_____
_____
_____

117. What's the most beautiful video you've ever experienced?
You: _____
_____
_____
_____

Your spouse: _____
_____
_____
_____

118. What is something you read or heard that has stuck with you for a long time?
    You: _____
    _____
    _____
    _____

    Your spouse: _____
    _____
    _____
    _____

119. What's your favorite thing to shop for, why?
    You: _____
    _____
    _____
    _____

    Your spouse: _____
    _____
    _____
    _____

120. What is the most ridiculous rule you have to follow?
    You: _____
    _____
    _____
    _____

    Your spouse: _____
    _____
    _____
    _____

121. *What bullet have you most recently dodged?*
　　 You: _____
　　 _____
　　 _____

　　 Your spouse: _____
　　 _____
　　 _____

122. *What do you have a hard time with that most people find easy?*
　　 You: _____
　　 _____
　　 _____

　　 Your spouse: _____
　　 _____
　　 _____

123. *If you could be an olympic athlete, what sport would you compete in?*
　　 You: _____
　　 _____
　　 _____

　　 Your spouse: _____
　　 _____
　　 _____

124. *What do you think is the greatest invention of all time?*
You: _____
_____
_____

Your spouse: _____
_____
_____

125. *What can you do today that you couldn't do a year ago?*
You: _____
_____
_____

Your spouse: _____
_____
_____

126. *If you were alone for 6 months, what would you do to stay sane?*
You: _____
_____
_____

Your spouse: _____
_____
_____

127. If you had to give up alcohol or coffee, what would you choose?
    You: _____
    _____
    _____

    Your spouse: _____
    _____
    _____

128. If you were the only human left on earth, what would you do first?
    You: _____
    _____
    _____

    Your spouse: _____
    _____
    _____

129. What's the highest thing on your bucket list?
    You: _____
    _____
    _____

    Your spouse: _____
    _____
    _____

130. *If you had to give a TED talk tomorrow, what would it be about?*

You: _____
_____
_____
_____

Your spouse: _____
_____
_____
_____

131. *If you could steal intelligence or talent from another person, who would you choose?*

You: _____
_____
_____
_____

Your spouse: _____
_____
_____
_____

132. *What's the best $20 you've ever spent?*

You: _____
_____
_____
_____

Your spouse: _____
_____
_____
_____

133. *What's something you always wanted to do as a child but never got to do?*
You: _____
_____
_____
_____

Your spouse: _____
_____
_____
_____

134. *Describe the worst haircut you've ever had...*
You: _____
_____
_____
_____

Your spouse: _____
_____
_____
_____

135. *What's the worst job you ever had?*
You: _____
_____
_____
_____

Your spouse: _____
_____
_____
_____

136. What fashion trend do you wish would go away?
    You: _____
    _____
    _____

    Your spouse: _____
    _____
    _____

137. What's your proudest moment?
    You: _____
    _____
    _____

    Your spouse: _____
    _____
    _____

138. What's the scariest thing you've ever done for fun?
    You: _____
    _____
    _____

    Your spouse: _____
    _____
    _____

139. If you could live in any TV show, which would it be?
    You: _____

    Your spouse: _____

140. If you had your own talk show, who would your first guests be?
    You: _____

    Your spouse: _____

141. If you could instantly become an expert in something, would would it be?
    You: _____

    Your spouse: _____

142. What childish things do you still do as an adult?
　　　You: _____
　　　_____
　　　_____
　　　_____

　　　Your spouse: _____
　　　_____
　　　_____
　　　_____

143. If you had one extra hour of free time a day, how would you use it?
　　　You: _____
　　　_____
　　　_____
　　　_____

　　　Your spouse: _____
　　　_____
　　　_____
　　　_____

144. If you could get rid of one thing in the world what would it be?
　　　You: _____
　　　_____
　　　_____
　　　_____

　　　Your spouse: _____
　　　_____
　　　_____
　　　_____

145. *What is something that you can do better than anyone else you know?*
    You: _____
    _____
    _____

    Your spouse: _____
    _____
    _____

146. *Would you rather have a rewind or pause button on your life?*
    You: _____
    _____
    _____

    Your spouse: _____
    _____
    _____

147. *What is your favorite spot in our home?*
    You: _____
    _____
    _____

    Your spouse: _____
    _____
    _____

148. What is the location of our most memorable kiss?
    You: _____
    _____
    _____

    Your spouse: _____
    _____
    _____

149. What is the movie I quote the most from?
    You: _____
    _____
    _____

    Your spouse: _____
    _____
    _____

150. What's the purchase you most regret?
    You: _____
    _____
    _____

    Your spouse: _____
    _____
    _____

151. A belonging of yours I'd get rid of if I could?
You: _____
_____
_____
_____

Your spouse: _____
_____
_____
_____

152. My least favorite household chore?
You: _____
_____
_____
_____

Your spouse: _____
_____
_____
_____

153. The social commitment I'd love to get out of?
You: _____
_____
_____
_____

Your spouse: _____
_____
_____
_____

154. *What I love most about your family?*
    You: _____
    _____
    _____
    _____

    Your spouse: _____
    _____
    _____
    _____

155. *The tv parent I want to be the most like?*
    You: _____
    _____
    _____
    _____

    Your spouse: _____
    _____
    _____
    _____

156. *The first music tape/CD you ever bought?*
    You: _____
    _____
    _____
    _____

    Your spouse: _____
    _____
    _____
    _____

157. *My favorite thing we've bought together...*
You: _____

Your spouse: _____

158. *What's the most unpleasant sounding word?*
You: _____

Your spouse: _____

159. *What is something weird you recommend everyone tries at least once?*
You: _____

Your spouse: _____

160. *What is the strangest thing you find attractive in someone?*
You: _____
_____
_____

Your spouse: _____
_____
_____

161. *If you were the opposite gender for a day what would be the first thing you do?*
You: _____
_____
_____

Your spouse: _____
_____
_____

162. *Do you have any superstitions?*
You: _____
_____
_____

Your spouse: _____
_____
_____

163. *Would you rather be the smartest or the most popular?*
    You: _____
    _____
    _____

    Your spouse: _____
    _____
    _____

164. *What's your grossest personal habit?*
    You: _____
    _____
    _____

    Your spouse: _____
    _____
    _____

165. *What's one thing you wish you could unsee?*
    You: _____
    _____
    _____

    Your spouse: _____
    _____
    _____

166. What event from your past would you like to relive?
    You: _____
    _____
    _____
    _____

    Your spouse: _____
    _____
    _____
    _____

167. What are 3 happiest moments from your life?
    You: _____
    _____
    _____
    _____

    Your spouse: _____
    _____
    _____
    _____

168. What talent of yours could you get paid to teach others?
    You: _____
    _____
    _____
    _____

    Your spouse: _____
    _____
    _____
    _____

169. *What is one goal you are still working to achieve?*
　　You: _____
　　_____
　　_____

　　Your spouse: _____
　　_____
　　_____

170. *What is your dream car?*
　　You: _____
　　_____
　　_____

　　Your spouse: _____
　　_____
　　_____

171. *What was your most interesting road trip ever?*
　　You: _____
　　_____
　　_____

　　Your spouse: _____
　　_____
　　_____

172. *What movie did you watch when you were too young?*
    You: _____
    _____
    _____
    _____

    Your spouse: _____
    _____
    _____
    _____

173. *How old were you when someone first told you about sex?*
    You: _____
    _____
    _____
    _____

    Your spouse: _____
    _____
    _____
    _____

174. *Which parent and grandparent of yours are you most like?*
    You: _____
    _____
    _____
    _____

    Your spouse: _____
    _____
    _____
    _____

175. What's the farthest you've ever walked?
You: _____
_____
_____

Your spouse: _____
_____
_____

176. What is an activity you used to enjoy that we don't do anymore but you'd like to start again?
You: _____
_____
_____

Your spouse: _____
_____
_____

177. Would you like to be famous? How so?
You: _____
_____
_____

Your spouse: _____
_____
_____

178. *Do you sing to yourself? What song?*
You: _____
_____
_____
_____

Your spouse: _____
_____
_____
_____

179. *What would be the perfect day for you?*
You: _____
_____
_____
_____

Your spouse: _____
_____
_____
_____

180. *Would you rather be too hot or too cold?*
You: _____
_____
_____
_____

Your spouse: _____
_____
_____
_____

181. Would you rather have a guaranteed $100,000 or a 50/50 shot at 1 million?

You: _____

Your spouse: _____

182. Would you rather have your first child in your 40s or as a teenager?

You: _____

Your spouse: _____

183. Would you rather lose $1000 or all of your phone contacts?

You: _____

Your spouse: _____

184. Would you rather be a horrible dancer or a horrible singer?
You: _____
_____
_____
_____

Your spouse: _____
_____
_____
_____

185. What is something you did as a child that your parents don't know about?
You: _____
_____
_____
_____

Your spouse: _____
_____
_____
_____

186. What is the best thing in your life right now? What is the hardest thing?
You: _____
_____
_____
_____

Your spouse: _____
_____
_____
_____

187. What was your favorite job in high school/college? Who were the people you worked with?
You: _____
_____
_____
_____

Your spouse: _____
_____
_____
_____

188. What made you laugh today?
You: _____
_____
_____
_____

Your spouse: _____
_____
_____
_____

189. What do you love most about being a parent?
You: _____
_____
_____
_____

Your spouse: _____
_____
_____
_____

190. What is your favorite outdoor activity? Why do you love it?
You: _____
_____
_____
_____

Your spouse: _____
_____
_____
_____

191. What frustrated you today? How did you deal with it?
You: _____
_____
_____
_____

Your spouse: _____
_____
_____
_____

192. Would you rather see the past or change the future?
You: _____
_____
_____
_____

Your spouse: _____
_____
_____
_____

193. *Who was your childhood hero?*
Your: _____
_____
_____

Your spouse: _____
_____
_____

194. *What was your biggest fear as a child?*
You: _____
_____
_____

Your spouse: _____
_____
_____

195. *What is your biggest fear now?*
You: _____
_____
_____

Your spouse: _____
_____
_____

196. *What is your favorite memory of us dating?*
You: _____
_____
_____
_____

Your spouse: _____
_____
_____
_____

197. *Who was the worst teacher you ever had?*
You: _____
_____
_____
_____

Your spouse: _____
_____
_____
_____

198. *Do you believe in ghosts or the supernatural?*
You: _____
_____
_____
_____

Your spouse: _____
_____
_____
_____

199. *How many dates would you like to go on to feel connected?*
You: _____
_____
_____

Your spouse: _____
_____
_____

200. *What is your favorite outfit that I wear?*
You: _____
_____
_____

Your spouse: _____
_____
_____

201. *What do you find most attractive about me?*
You: _____
_____
_____

Your spouse: _____
_____
_____

202. *I'm way too competitive about...*
You: _____
_____
_____
_____

Your spouse: _____
_____
_____
_____

203. *What would your last meal be?*
You: _____
_____
_____
_____

Your spouse: _____
_____
_____
_____

204. *Would you rather live in a beach house or cozy mountain cabin?*
You: _____
_____
_____
_____

Your spouse: _____
_____
_____
_____

205. Would you rather donate to charity or go volunteer in person to those in need?

You: _____

Your spouse: _____

206. Are you restless when there isn't anything to do or relaxed?

You: _____

Your spouse: _____

207. Do you like social gatherings? Or do you feel like your energy is spent when you get home?

You: _____

Your spouse: _____

208. *If you could own any small business, what would it be?*
You: _____
_____
_____
_____

Your spouse: _____
_____
_____
_____

209. *What do you dislike more? A messy home or spending the day cleaning?*
You: _____
_____
_____
_____

Your spouse: _____
_____
_____
_____

210. *Do you enjoy making lists?*
You: _____
_____
_____

Your spouse: _____
_____
_____
_____

211. Do you think before responding to text messages or do you respond right away?
    You: _____

    Your spouse: _____

212. Would you rather wear boots or flip flops for the rest of your life?
    You: _____

    Your spouse: _____

213. How long does it take you to get ready in the morning?
    You: _____

    Your spouse: _____

214. What stresses you out when traveling?
You:

Your spouse:

215. Who was your favorite family member growing up?
You:

Your spouse:

216. Have you ever had an enemy?
You:

Your spouse:

217. What is the scariest story you've ever heard?
   You: _____
   _____
   _____

   Your spouse: _____
   _____
   _____

218. What song reminds you of me?
   You: _____
   _____
   _____

   Your spouse: _____
   _____
   _____

219. Who is your favorite cousin, aunt/uncle?
   You: _____
   _____
   _____

   Your spouse: _____
   _____
   _____

220. What is your earliest happy memory?
You: _____
_____
_____

Your spouse: _____
_____
_____

221. What is your earliest scary memory?
You: _____
_____
_____

Your spouse: _____
_____
_____

222. What is the first memory you have?
You: _____
_____
_____

Your spouse: _____
_____
_____

223. *If you won the lottery would you continue working?*
    You: _____
    _____
    _____
    _____

    Your spouse: _____
    _____
    _____
    _____

224. *What kind of sports do you enjoy and why?*
    You: _____
    _____
    _____
    _____

    Your spouse: _____
    _____
    _____
    _____

225. *What kind of movies do you enjoy and why?*
    You: _____
    _____
    _____
    _____

    Your spouse: _____
    _____
    _____
    _____

226. What animals do you like?
    You: _____
    _____
    _____
    _____

    Your spouse: _____
    _____
    _____
    _____

227. What animals do you dislike?
    You: _____
    _____
    _____
    _____

    Your spouse: _____
    _____
    _____
    _____

228. Who is your favorite actress?
    You: _____
    _____
    _____
    _____

    Your spouse: _____
    _____
    _____
    _____

229. *Which celebrity would you dream to meet?*
　　You: _____
　　_____
　　_____

　　Your spouse: _____
　　_____
　　_____

230. *Who is your favorite actor?*
　　You: _____
　　_____
　　_____

　　Your spouse: _____
　　_____
　　_____

231. *What celebrity wardrobe do you wish you could have?*
　　You: _____
　　_____
　　_____

　　Your spouse: _____
　　_____
　　_____

232. Would you rather an extra hour of sleep or alone time?
You: _____
_____
_____

Your spouse: _____
_____
_____

233. Would you rather have another baby or another pet?
You: _____
_____
_____

Your spouse: _____
_____
_____

234. Would you rather drive for hours or work in the yard for hours?
You: _____
_____
_____

Your spouse: _____
_____
_____

235. *What were your favorite things to do 10 years ago?*
You: _____
_____
_____
_____

Your spouse: _____
_____
_____
_____

236. *If money wasn't an issue, how would you spend your time?*
You: _____
_____
_____
_____

Your spouse: _____
_____
_____
_____

237. *How did you get to school when you were little?*
You: _____
_____
_____
_____

Your spouse: _____
_____
_____
_____

238. Who was your childhood celebrity crush?
You: _____
_____
_____
_____

Your spouse: _____
_____
_____
_____

239. How did your parents help you when you were sick?
You: _____
_____
_____
_____

Your spouse: _____
_____
_____
_____

240. What did you watch on TV when you were little?
You: _____
_____
_____
_____

Your spouse: _____
_____
_____
_____

241. Did you babysit? Tell me a story from babysitting?
    You: _____
    _____
    _____
    _____

    Your spouse: _____
    _____
    _____
    _____

242. What clothes did your parents make you wear that you hated?
    You: _____
    _____
    _____
    _____

    Your spouse: _____
    _____
    _____
    _____

243. What was your worst hairstyle?
    You: _____
    _____
    _____
    _____

    Your spouse: _____
    _____
    _____
    _____

244. What was your most memorable child birthday party?
You: _____
_____
_____
_____

Your spouse: _____
_____
_____
_____

245. What was the naughtiest thing you did as a child/teen?
You: _____
_____
_____
_____

Your spouse: _____
_____
_____
_____

246. Who was the first person to break your heart?
You: _____
_____
_____
_____

Your spouse: _____
_____
_____
_____

247. What would the soundtrack to your teenage years be?
You: _____
_____
_____
_____

Your spouse: _____
_____
_____
_____

248. Who was your first kiss with and what was it like?
You: _____
_____
_____
_____

Your spouse: _____
_____
_____
_____

249. Who taught you to drive and what was your worst driving experience?
You: _____
_____
_____
_____

Your spouse: _____
_____
_____
_____

250. What sports/clubs were you a part of?
You: _____
_____
_____
_____

Your spouse: _____
_____
_____
_____

251. If you could create a scent, what would it smell like?
You: _____
_____
_____
_____

Your spouse: _____
_____
_____
_____

252. If you could never do this one chore every again, what would it be?
You: _____
_____
_____
_____

Your spouse: _____
_____
_____
_____

253. *If you could ask G-d a question, what would you ask?*
You: _____
_____
_____

Your spouse: _____
_____
_____

254. *When you think of a home, what do you imagine?*
You: _____
_____
_____

Your spouse: _____
_____
_____

255. *What makes you feel most peaceful?*
You: _____
_____
_____

Your spouse: _____
_____
_____

256. Do you love sunrises or sunsets better?
    You: _____

    Your spouse: _____

257. What feature of yours makes you feel the most self conscious?
    You: _____

    Your spouse: _____

258. What TV show do you wish I would stop watching?
    You: _____

    Your spouse: _____

259. What is the kindest thing you've ever done for someone else?
    You: _____
    _____
    _____
    _____

    Your spouse: _____
    _____
    _____
    _____

260. What is your personal motto you live by?
    You: _____
    _____
    _____
    _____

    Your spouse: _____
    _____
    _____
    _____

261. What is your favorite memory of us together?
    You: _____
    _____
    _____
    _____

    Your spouse: _____
    _____
    _____
    _____

262. What is the last time I did something that surprised you?
    You: _____
    _____
    _____
    _____

    Your spouse: _____
    _____
    _____
    _____

263. What's your favorite thing to do on a weekend morning?
    You: _____
    _____
    _____
    _____

    Your spouse: _____
    _____
    _____
    _____

264. If we could jump in the car right now and take a road trip, where would you want to go?
    You: _____
    _____
    _____
    _____

    Your spouse: _____
    _____
    _____
    _____

265. *What would your dream house look like?*
    You: _____
    _____
    _____
    _____

    Your spouse: _____
    _____
    _____
    _____

266. *What movements are you passionate about?*
    You: _____
    _____
    _____
    _____

    Your spouse: _____
    _____
    _____
    _____

267. *What is your wildest dream?*
    You: _____
    _____
    _____
    _____

    Your spouse: _____
    _____
    _____
    _____

268. *What are you doing to pursue your dreams?*
You: _____
_____
_____

Your spouse: _____
_____
_____

269. *How can I be involved in your dreams?*
You: _____
_____
_____

Your spouse: _____
_____
_____

270. *Where do you feel most inspired?*
You: _____
_____
_____

Your spouse: _____
_____
_____

271. *What do you hope for us in our relationships in the next year?*
    You: _____
    _____
    _____
    _____

    Your spouse: _____
    _____
    _____
    _____

272. *What is the most meaningful thing we've accomplished together?*
    You: _____
    _____
    _____
    _____

    Your spouse: _____
    _____
    _____
    _____

273. *Can we have both a dream job and a dream marriage?*
    You: _____
    _____
    _____
    _____

    Your spouse: _____
    _____
    _____
    _____

274. Do you believe it's possible to have platonic relationships?
You: _____
_____
_____
_____

Your spouse: _____
_____
_____
_____

275. Do you live to work or work to live or neither?
You: _____
_____
_____
_____

Your spouse: _____
_____
_____
_____

276. Would you prefer to work in the morning or at night if you could design your own schedule?
You: _____
_____
_____
_____

Your spouse: _____
_____
_____
_____

277. Would you rather have the best house in a bad neighborhood or the worst house in a good neighborhood?
You: _____
_____
_____
_____

Your spouse: _____
_____
_____
_____

278. What's a fun memory you have of me wearing a certain outfit?
You: _____
_____
_____
_____

Your spouse: _____
_____
_____
_____

279. I like it best when you refer to me as...
You: _____
_____
_____
_____

Your spouse: _____
_____
_____
_____

280. The song that makes me think of you is...
    You: _____
    _____
    _____

    Your spouse: _____
    _____
    _____

281. If I had to do it again, I would propose to you by?
    You: _____
    _____
    _____

    Your spouse: _____
    _____
    _____

282. My favorite photo of us is?
    You: _____
    _____
    _____

    Your spouse: _____
    _____
    _____

283. *I feel you love me the most when...*
    You: _____
    _____
    _____
    _____

    Your spouse: _____
    _____
    _____
    _____

284. *I get scared when...*
    You: _____
    _____
    _____
    _____

    Your spouse: _____
    _____
    _____
    _____

285. *If we could do our honeymoon over again, how would we do it?*
    You: _____
    _____
    _____
    _____

    Your spouse: _____
    _____
    _____
    _____

286. When was the first moment you knew I was the one?
    You: _____
    _____
    _____
    _____

    Your spouse: _____
    _____
    _____
    _____

287. What makes you the happiest?
    You: _____
    _____
    _____
    _____

    Your spouse: _____
    _____
    _____
    _____

288. What kind of physical touch makes you feel most loved?
    You: _____
    _____
    _____
    _____

    Your spouse: _____
    _____
    _____
    _____

289. What was the strangest punishment your parents ever gave you?
You: _____
_____
_____

Your spouse: _____
_____
_____

290. If you were arrested, what would it be for?
You: _____
_____
_____

Your spouse: _____
_____
_____

291. What is your favorite thing to do alone?
You: _____
_____
_____

Your spouse: _____
_____
_____

292. *If I could do one thing every day to make your life easier/happier, what would it be?*
You: _____
_____
_____
_____

Your spouse: _____
_____
_____
_____

293. *What's the funniest thing you've heard our kids say lately?*
You: _____
_____
_____
_____

Your spouse: _____
_____
_____
_____

294. *What's something about me that makes you smile?*
You: _____
_____
_____
_____

Your spouse: _____
_____
_____
_____

295. *What are three things on your bucket list?*
    You: _____
    _____
    _____

    Your spouse: _____
    _____
    _____

Next Section

Relationship Questions
Medium Level of intensity

1. *What have you been interested in or learning about lately?*
   You: _____
   _____
   _____

   Your spouse: _____
   _____
   _____

2. *What is the one thing we have argued the most about in the past 90 days?*
   You: _____
   _____
   _____

   Your spouse: _____
   _____
   _____

3. *When do you feel respected by me?*
   You: _____
   _____
   _____

   Your spouse: _____
   _____
   _____

4. Which couple do you look up to the most and why?
   You: _____
   _____
   _____

   Your spouse: _____
   _____
   _____

5. What is something I do that makes you feel loved the most?
   You: _____
   _____
   _____

   Your spouse: _____
   _____
   _____

6. What is your first memory of me? Describe it in detail...
   You: _____
   _____
   _____

   Your spouse: _____
   _____
   _____

7. *What do you want the atmosphere in our home to feel like?*
   You: _____
   _____
   _____

   Your spouse: _____
   _____
   _____

8. *What person or people had the most impact on your life and how?*
   You: _____
   _____
   _____

   Your spouse: _____
   _____
   _____

9. *What do you do to get yourself in a better mood when you are not feeling great?*
   You: _____
   _____
   _____

   Your spouse: _____
   _____
   _____

10. What would you do if I changed my religious beliefs?
    You: _____
    _____
    _____
    _____

    Your spouse: _____
    _____
    _____
    _____

11. How do you feel about supporting family members financially?
    You: _____
    _____
    _____
    _____

    Your spouse: _____
    _____
    _____
    _____

12. What are 3 physical shows of affection you really enjoy from me and wish I would do more often?
    You: _____
    _____
    _____
    _____

    Your spouse: _____
    _____
    _____
    _____

13. *Do you have any trouble opening up and talking with me?*
    You: _____
    _____
    _____

    Your spouse: _____
    _____
    _____

14. *Describe yourself in 3 words...*
    You: _____
    _____
    _____

    Your spouse: _____
    _____
    _____

15. *Describe your partner in 3 words...*
    You: _____
    _____
    _____

    Your spouse: _____
    _____
    _____

16. *What is one thing you want to do differently than your parents?*
    You: _____
    _____
    _____
    _____

    Your spouse: _____
    _____
    _____
    _____

17. *What is your favorite memory of us?*
    You: _____
    _____
    _____
    _____

    Your spouse: _____
    _____
    _____
    _____

18. *What are your goals this year?*
    You: _____
    _____
    _____
    _____

    Your spouse: _____
    _____
    _____
    _____

19. What in your life are you most grateful for?
    You: _____
    _____
    _____
    _____

    Your spouse: _____
    _____
    _____
    _____

20. What are 3 ways I make you feel the most loved?
    You: _____
    _____
    _____
    _____

    Your spouse: _____
    _____
    _____
    _____

21. What do you think is the #1 thing that makes a relationship last?
    You: _____
    _____
    _____
    _____

    Your spouse: _____
    _____
    _____
    _____

22. What things are you afraid of?
    You: _____
    _____
    _____
    _____

    Your spouse: _____
    _____
    _____
    _____

23. If you had the chance to rewrite a moment in your life what would it be?
    You: _____
    _____
    _____
    _____

    Your spouse: _____
    _____
    _____
    _____

24. What do you consider your greatest accomplishment thus far?
    You: _____
    _____
    _____
    _____

    Your spouse: _____
    _____
    _____
    _____

25. *What do you hope to accomplish by the time you retire?*
    You: _____
    _____
    _____

    Your spouse: _____
    _____
    _____

26. *What do you hope to accomplish by the time you die?*
    You: _____
    _____
    _____

    Your spouse: _____
    _____
    _____

27. *What do you admire most about your mom?*
    You: _____
    _____
    _____

    Your spouse: _____
    _____
    _____

28. What do you admire most about your dad?
    You: _____
    _____
    _____
    _____

    Your spouse: _____
    _____
    _____
    _____

29. What is one character trait you want to pass on to your kids?
    You: _____
    _____
    _____
    _____

    Your spouse: _____
    _____
    _____
    _____

30. What is one character trait you hope your kids don't learn from you?
    You: _____
    _____
    _____
    _____

    Your spouse: _____
    _____
    _____
    _____

31. *If you could pick a career for each of our children what would it be?*
   You: _____
   _____
   _____
   _____

   Your spouse: _____
   _____
   _____
   _____

32. *What was the nicest thing anyone has said to you?*
   You: _____
   _____
   _____
   _____

   Your spouse: _____
   _____
   _____
   _____

33. *What is your relationship with your siblings like?*
   You: _____
   _____
   _____
   _____

   Your spouse: _____
   _____
   _____
   _____

34. What is your biggest worry?
    You: _____
    _____
    _____
    _____

    Your spouse: _____
    _____
    _____
    _____

35. What is something you're waiting for?
    You: _____
    _____
    _____
    _____

    Your spouse: _____
    _____
    _____
    _____

36. How do you describe your relationship with your parents?
    You: _____
    _____
    _____
    _____

    Your spouse: _____
    _____
    _____
    _____

37. What is something you should have said a long time ago?
    You: _____
    _____
    _____
    _____

    Your spouse: _____
    _____
    _____
    _____

38. Which world culture is most interesting to you?
    You: _____
    _____
    _____
    _____

    Your spouse: _____
    _____
    _____
    _____

39. Do you think the way we dress affects how we think?
    You: _____
    _____
    _____
    _____

    Your spouse: _____
    _____
    _____
    _____

40. Which is more important: the human body or the human mind?
　　You: _____
　　_____
　　_____

　　Your spouse: _____
　　_____
　　_____

41. What have you been most proud of learning lately?
　　You: _____
　　_____
　　_____

　　Your spouse: _____
　　_____
　　_____

42. Do you think people have a higher calling in life?
　　You: _____
　　_____
　　_____

　　Your spouse: _____
　　_____
　　_____

43. What are two of the biggest lessons you've learned from previous relationships?
    You: _____
    _____
    _____

    Your spouse: _____
    _____
    _____

44. What would be the perfect day?
    You: _____
    _____
    _____

    Your spouse: _____
    _____
    _____

45. What did you learn a little too late?
    You: _____
    _____
    _____

    Your spouse: _____
    _____
    _____

46. What unhygenic things do people do that bother you?
    You: _____
    _____
    _____
    _____

    Your spouse: _____
    _____
    _____
    _____

47. What habit do you have that annoys other people?
    You: _____
    _____
    _____
    _____

    Your spouse: _____
    _____
    _____
    _____

48. What are you too hard on yourself for?
    You: _____
    _____
    _____
    _____

    Your spouse: _____
    _____
    _____
    _____

49. *What habit do you have that not many other people have?*
You: _____
_____
_____

Your spouse: _____
_____
_____

50. *What do most people overestimate or underestimate about you?*
You: _____
_____
_____

Your spouse: _____
_____
_____

51. *How often do you feel utterly worn down?*
You: _____
_____
_____

Your spouse: _____
_____
_____

52. What is something you should do but will probably never do?
    You: _____
    _____
    _____

    Your spouse: _____
    _____
    _____

53. What is the best thing about how you were raised?
    You: _____
    _____
    _____

    Your spouse: _____
    _____
    _____

54. What is the worst thing about how you were raised?
    You: _____
    _____
    _____

    Your spouse: _____
    _____
    _____

55. *What do you look forward to about getting old?*
    You: _____
    _____
    _____

    Your spouse: _____
    _____
    _____

56. *What is something you tried really hard to like but couldn't?*
    You: _____
    _____
    _____

    Your spouse: _____
    _____
    _____

57. *What makes you different from most people?*
    You: _____
    _____
    _____

    Your spouse: _____
    _____
    _____

58. *What was the best mistake you've ever made?*
    You: _____
    _____
    _____
    _____

    Your spouse: _____
    _____
    _____
    _____

59. *Who was the most toxic person you've ever known?*
    You: _____
    _____
    _____
    _____

    Your spouse: _____
    _____
    _____
    _____

60. *What makes you nervous?*
    You: _____
    _____
    _____
    _____

    Your spouse: _____
    _____
    _____
    _____

61. *What makes you angrier than it should?*
    You: _____
    _____
    _____
    _____

    Your spouse: _____
    _____
    _____
    _____

62. *What was the last time you felt jealous and why?*
    You: _____
    _____
    _____
    _____

    Your spouse: _____
    _____
    _____
    _____

63. *What memory do you want to keep from today?*
    You: _____
    _____
    _____
    _____

    Your spouse: _____
    _____
    _____
    _____

64. *What makes you sweat?*
   You: _____

   Your spouse: _____

65. *What do you wish your job was?*
   You: _____

   Your spouse: _____

66. *What are you passionate about?*
   You: _____

   Your spouse: _____

67. *Are you holding a grudge?*
You: _____
_____
_____

Your spouse: _____
_____
_____

68. *Were you positive or negative today?*
You: _____
_____
_____

Your spouse: _____
_____
_____

69. *Who is the strongest person you know?*
You: _____
_____
_____

Your spouse: _____
_____
_____

70. *Who do you wish had been a part of your day?*
    You: _____
    _____
    _____
    _____

    Your spouse: _____
    _____
    _____
    _____

71. *What is one thing you were told today you don't want to forget?*
    You: _____
    _____
    _____
    _____

    Your spouse: _____
    _____
    _____
    _____

72. *What's worth fighting for?*
    You: _____
    _____
    _____
    _____

    Your spouse: _____
    _____
    _____
    _____

73. *What improvements are you making?*
   You: _____
   _____
   _____

   Your spouse: _____
   _____
   _____

74. *What in life is beautiful to you, where do you find inspiration?*
   You: _____
   _____
   _____

   Your spouse: _____
   _____
   _____

75. *When did your life change for the better?*
   You: _____
   _____
   _____

   Your spouse: _____
   _____
   _____

76. *How do you manage stress?*
    You: _____
    _____
    _____
    _____

    Your spouse: _____
    _____
    _____
    _____

77. *What do you believe stands between you and complete happiness?*
    You: _____
    _____
    _____
    _____

    Your spouse: _____
    _____
    _____
    _____

78. *What's one thing you wish to accomplish before you die?*
    You: _____
    _____
    _____
    _____

    Your spouse: _____
    _____
    _____
    _____

79. What is something you think everyone should experience in their lifetime?
    You: _____
    _____
    _____

    Your spouse: _____
    _____
    _____

80. Is it easier to hate or love, why?
    You: _____
    _____
    _____

    Your spouse: _____
    _____
    _____

81. Do you think the end or the means is more important?
    You: _____
    _____
    _____

    Your spouse: _____
    _____
    _____

82. *What is your biggest passion?*
    You: _____
    _____
    _____
    _____

    Your spouse: _____
    _____
    _____
    _____

83. *Is there something you dreamed of doing for a long time? Why haven't you done it?*
    You: _____
    _____
    _____
    _____

    Your spouse: _____
    _____
    _____
    _____

84. *In one word what do you live for?*
    You: _____
    _____
    _____
    _____

    Your spouse: _____
    _____
    _____
    _____

85. *Are you afraid of being your true self around others? Why?*
    You: _____

    Your spouse: _____

86. *What is one little thing that I do for you that you appreciate?*
    You: _____

    Your spouse: _____

87. *What do you remember about your impression of me when we first met?*
    You: _____

    Your spouse: _____

88. What makes you most proud of me?
    You: _____
    _____
    _____
    _____

    Your spouse: _____
    _____
    _____
    _____

89. What is something in your past you would have liked me to see?
    You: _____
    _____
    _____
    _____

    Your spouse: _____
    _____
    _____
    _____

90. What is one word that describes me?
    You: _____
    _____
    _____
    _____

    Your spouse: _____
    _____
    _____
    _____

91. *Who is a high school friend you respected a lot?*
    You: _____

    Your spouse: _____

92. *What is your earliest memory in life?*
    You: _____

    Your spouse: _____

93. *What made you fall in love with me?*
    You: _____

    Your spouse: _____

94. What are 3 of the most important choices you've made so far in your life?
   You: _____
   _____
   _____
   _____

   Your spouse: _____
   _____
   _____
   _____

95. What is the best piece of advice you've ever been given?
   You: _____
   _____
   _____
   _____

   Your spouse: _____
   _____
   _____
   _____

96. What is one of our traditions that you especially like?
   You: _____
   _____
   _____
   _____

   Your spouse: _____
   _____
   _____
   _____

97. *How do you describe me to other people?*
    You: _____

    Your spouse: _____

98. *Who is someone in your past you would have liked me to meet?*
    You: _____

    Your spouse: _____

99. *How do you show someone you love them?*
    You: _____

    Your spouse: _____

100. *What small or large event changed your life the most?*
You: _____

Your spouse: _____

101. *What do you have a hard time taking seriously?*
You: _____

Your spouse: _____

102. *What do you judge people for most often?*
You: _____

Your spouse: _____

103. *What's the best compliment that someone can receive?*
You: _____
_____
_____

Your spouse: _____
_____
_____

104. *What's something you can do that most people can't?*
You: _____
_____
_____

Your spouse: _____
_____
_____

105. *How do you calm yourself down when you are angry?*
You: _____
_____
_____

Your spouse: _____
_____
_____

106. When was the last time you tried to look cool and it ended in embarrassment?
You: _____

Your spouse: _____

107. Where do you want to live when we retire?
You: _____

Your spouse: _____

108. Where do you see yourself in 5 years?
You: _____

Your spouse: _____

109. *What was your greatest moment?*
You: _____
_____
_____

Your spouse: _____
_____
_____

110. *How has your place in the birth order in your family impacted you?*
You: _____
_____
_____

Your spouse: _____
_____
_____

111. *How would you spend your 100th birthday?*
You: _____
_____
_____

Your spouse: _____
_____
_____

112. *What's the strangest dream you ever had?*
    You: _____
    _____
    _____
    _____

    Your spouse: _____
    _____
    _____
    _____

113. *What do you pray about?*
    You: _____
    _____
    _____
    _____

    Your spouse: _____
    _____
    _____
    _____

114. *What's the highest level of pain you've ever been in, on a scale of 0-10?*
    You: _____
    _____
    _____
    _____

    Your spouse: _____
    _____
    _____
    _____

115. What's the best gift anyone has ever given to you?
    You: _____
    _____
    _____
    _____

    Your spouse: _____
    _____
    _____
    _____

116. If you could eliminate one thing from your daily routine, what would it be?
    You: _____
    _____
    _____
    _____

    Your spouse: _____
    _____
    _____
    _____

117. One thing I still hope to achieve in my life?
    You: _____
    _____
    _____
    _____

    Your spouse: _____
    _____
    _____
    _____

118. Qualities I admire most about others...
　　　You: _____
　　　_____
　　　_____
　　　_____

　　　Your spouse: _____
　　　_____
　　　_____
　　　_____

119. Where do you go when you want to be alone?
　　　You: _____
　　　_____
　　　_____
　　　_____

　　　Your spouse: _____
　　　_____
　　　_____
　　　_____

120. What are some selfless acts people have done to make your life better?
　　　You: _____
　　　_____
　　　_____
　　　_____

　　　Your spouse: _____
　　　_____
　　　_____
　　　_____

121. Have you ever done anything wild that you still enjoy when you think about it?

You: _____

_____

_____

Your spouse: _____

_____

_____

122. What are some morals you live by?

You: _____

_____

_____

Your spouse: _____

_____

_____

123. What are you tired of hearing about?

You: _____

_____

_____

Your spouse: _____

_____

_____

124. What's the biggest secret you've kept from your parents?
    You: _____
    _____
    _____
    _____

    Your spouse: _____
    _____
    _____
    _____

125. What would you say if you had to pretend to like a present?
    You: _____
    _____
    _____
    _____

    Your spouse: _____
    _____
    _____
    _____

126. What does husband/wife material mean to you?
    You: _____
    _____
    _____
    _____

    Your spouse: _____
    _____
    _____
    _____

127. What are 5 things you'd tell your 15 year old self?
You: _____
_____
_____
_____

Your spouse: _____
_____
_____
_____

128. What are 5 things that make you happy?
You: _____
_____
_____
_____

Your spouse: _____
_____
_____
_____

129. What popular notion do you think the world has most wrong?
You: _____
_____
_____
_____

Your spouse: _____
_____
_____
_____

130. What is your first memory of me?
    You: _____
    _____
    _____
    _____

    Your spouse: _____
    _____
    _____
    _____

131. If money were no object, what would you do for the rest of your life?
    You: _____
    _____
    _____
    _____

    Your spouse: _____
    _____
    _____
    _____

132. If I could meet only one of your needs, which one would it be?
    You: _____
    _____
    _____
    _____

    Your spouse: _____
    _____
    _____
    _____

133. *What surprised you the most about having children?*
 You: _____
 _____
 _____
 _____

 Your spouse: _____
 _____
 _____
 _____

134. *What is your dream for your life and our family?*
 You: _____
 _____
 _____
 _____

 Your spouse: _____
 _____
 _____
 _____

135. *What do you miss about our life before children?*
 You: _____
 _____
 _____
 _____

 Your spouse: _____
 _____
 _____
 _____

136. *What is your favorite activity that we do together?*
You: _____
_____
_____
_____

Your spouse: _____
_____
_____
_____

137. *What is a characteristic that you have that is under-appreciated?*
You: _____
_____
_____
_____

Your spouse: _____
_____
_____
_____

138. *What do I say that makes you feel disrespected?*
You: _____
_____
_____
_____

Your spouse: _____
_____
_____
_____

139. *What is something you wish your spouse did better?*
    You: _____
    _____
    _____
    _____

    Your spouse: _____
    _____
    _____
    _____

140. *What is your spouse's most difficult challenge?*
    You: _____
    _____
    _____
    _____

    Your spouse: _____
    _____
    _____
    _____

141. *When you were growing up, how did you see love expressed in your home?*
    You: _____
    _____
    _____
    _____

    Your spouse: _____
    _____
    _____
    _____

142. Was affection openly expressed?
    You: _____
    _____
    _____
    _____

    Your spouse: _____
    _____
    _____
    _____

143. How were birthdays and holidays celebrated in your home?
    You: _____
    _____
    _____
    _____

    Your spouse: _____
    _____
    _____
    _____

144. How was family time managed in your home. Was it consistent or done at random?
    You: _____
    _____
    _____
    _____

    Your spouse: _____
    _____
    _____
    _____

145. *What kind of verbal encouragement did you hear growing up. Who gave it the most?*
    You: _____
    _____
    _____
    _____

    Your spouse: _____
    _____
    _____
    _____

146. *What is the best gift you've ever given your spouse?*
    You: _____
    _____
    _____
    _____

    Your spouse: _____
    _____
    _____
    _____

147. *What would you love to hear your spouse say?*
    You: _____
    _____
    _____
    _____

    Your spouse: _____
    _____
    _____
    _____

148. What is one gift your spouse can give you that would make you feel their love?

You: _____

_____

_____

Your spouse: _____

_____

_____

149. What does quality time with your spouse mean to you? What do you do during this time?

You: _____

_____

_____

Your spouse: _____

_____

_____

150. What things are missing in your life now?

You: _____

_____

_____

Your spouse: _____

_____

_____

151. *How can we have more fun in our life?*
    You: _____
    _____
    _____
    _____

    Your spouse: _____
    _____
    _____
    _____

152. *If you could change one character trait about yourself, what would it be and why?*
    You: _____
    _____
    _____
    _____

    Your spouse: _____
    _____
    _____
    _____

153. *How have you changed in the last year?*
    You: _____
    _____
    _____
    _____

    Your spouse: _____
    _____
    _____
    _____

154. Who in your life is most stressful for you, why?
    You: _____
    _____
    _____
    _____

    Your spouse: _____
    _____
    _____
    _____

155. What were the highlights and lowlights of your childhood?
    You: _____
    _____
    _____
    _____

    Your spouse: _____
    _____
    _____
    _____

156. Where do you want to be in 3 years?
    You: _____
    _____
    _____
    _____

    Your spouse: _____
    _____
    _____
    _____

157. *What does the word romance mean to you?*
You: _____
_____
_____

Your spouse: _____
_____
_____

158. *What do you think I'm thinking?*
You: _____
_____
_____

Your spouse: _____
_____
_____

159. *What is something you never told your parents about until much later that now you both laugh about?*
You: _____
_____
_____

Your spouse: _____
_____
_____

160. What does success mean to you?
    You: _____

    Your spouse: _____

161. When was the last time you cried by yourself?
    You: _____

    Your spouse: _____

162. If you could wake up with one new quality or ability that you could gain overnight, what would you choose?
    You: _____

    Your spouse: _____

163. *If you could see into the future, what would you want to know?*
You: _____
_____
_____
_____

Your spouse: _____
_____
_____
_____

164. *Is there something you've dreamed of doing for a long time? Why haven't you done it yet?*
You: _____
_____
_____
_____

Your spouse: _____
_____
_____
_____

165. *What do you value most in a friendship?*
You: _____
_____
_____
_____

Your spouse: _____
_____
_____
_____

166. What is your most treasured memory?
    You: _____
    _____
    _____
    _____

    Your spouse: _____
    _____
    _____
    _____

167. What is your most terrible memory?
    You: _____
    _____
    _____
    _____

    Your spouse: _____
    _____
    _____
    _____

168. If you had one year to live, would you change anything about the way you are now living?
    You: _____
    _____
    _____
    _____

    Your spouse: _____
    _____
    _____
    _____

169. How close or warm is your family? Do you feel your childhood was happy?
    You: _____
    _____
    _____
    _____

    Your spouse: _____
    _____
    _____
    _____

170. How was your relationship with your mother?
    You: _____
    _____
    _____
    _____

    Your spouse: _____
    _____
    _____
    _____

171. What is something that's been on your mind the last week?
    You: _____
    _____
    _____
    _____

    Your spouse: _____
    _____
    _____
    _____

172. *When was the last time I made you laugh the most?*
 You: _____
 _____
 _____
 _____

 Your spouse: _____
 _____
 _____
 _____

173. *What is your biggest flaw?*
 You: _____
 _____
 _____
 _____

 Your spouse: _____
 _____
 _____
 _____

174. *Do you believe in soulmates?*
 You: _____
 _____
 _____
 _____

 Your spouse: _____
 _____
 _____
 _____

175. *Do you get enough time to hang out with your friends/family?*
    You: _____
    _____
    _____
    _____

    Your spouse: _____
    _____
    _____
    _____

176. *What are you most scared of right now?*
    You: _____
    _____
    _____
    _____

    Your spouse: _____
    _____
    _____
    _____

177. *What do you feel is missing in your life right now?*
    You: _____
    _____
    _____
    _____

    Your spouse: _____
    _____
    _____
    _____

178. What do you love most about yourself?
You: _____
_____
_____
_____

Your spouse: _____
_____
_____
_____

179. What do you dislike most about yourself?
You: _____
_____
_____
_____

Your spouse: _____
_____
_____
_____

180. How would you describe the ideal marriage?
You: _____
_____
_____
_____

Your spouse: _____
_____
_____
_____

181. *What ideas do we have that have helped us become a stronger couple?*
You: _____
_____
_____
_____

Your spouse: _____
_____
_____
_____

182. *What does love mean to you?*
You: _____
_____
_____
_____

Your spouse: _____
_____
_____
_____

183. *How can I make your day easier?*
You: _____
_____
_____
_____

Your spouse: _____
_____
_____
_____

184. When did you feel appreciated today?
You: _____

Your spouse: _____

185. What are you most likely to do to express your love to your significant other: clean the house, write a love note, buy a special gift, plan a fun date night, give a good foot massage?
You: _____

Your spouse: _____

186. Which of our marriage vows do you think are most important?
You: _____

Your spouse: _____

187. What would be the best gift I could give you?
You: _____

Your spouse: _____

188. What is the most romantic movie you've ever seen?
You: _____

Your spouse: _____

189. Tell me about your first crush.
You: _____

Your spouse: _____

190. What was your worst date ever?
You: _____
_____
_____
_____

Your spouse: _____
_____
_____
_____

191. When did your parents teach you about sex?
You: _____
_____
_____
_____

Your spouse: _____
_____
_____
_____

192. Do you like surprises or do you prefer making plans together?
You: _____
_____
_____
_____

Your spouse: _____
_____
_____
_____

193. *Do you believe in the afterlife?*
    You: _____
    _____
    _____

    Your spouse: _____
    _____
    _____

194. *What was the most life-changing event that you've ever experienced?*
    You: _____
    _____
    _____

    Your spouse: _____
    _____
    _____

195. *Do you believe pure happiness exists? Have you ever felt it?*
    You: _____
    _____
    _____

    Your spouse: _____
    _____
    _____

196. *How should we part at the beginning of each day? How would you like it to look when we first come home to each other?*

You: _____
_____
_____
_____

Your spouse: _____
_____
_____
_____

197. *What family rituals or traditions would you like for us to start?*

You: _____
_____
_____
_____

Your spouse: _____
_____
_____
_____

198. *What is your dream goal for our family?*

You: _____
_____
_____
_____

Your spouse: _____
_____
_____
_____

199. *What has occurred recently that is very important to you?*
    You: _____
    _____
    _____
    _____

    Your spouse: _____
    _____
    _____
    _____

200. *What was a recent triumph?*
    You: _____
    _____
    _____
    _____

    Your spouse: _____
    _____
    _____
    _____

201. *What are you looking forward to the most?*
    You: _____
    _____
    _____
    _____

    Your spouse: _____
    _____
    _____
    _____

202. What was your first impression of me?
You:

Your spouse:

203. Can you remember your parents fighting? What were they fighting about?
You:

Your spouse:

204. How do you think people perceive you? Do you think your perception is accurate?
You:

Your spouse:

205. *Who had control of the money when you were growing up?*
You: _____
_____
_____

Your spouse: _____
_____
_____

206. *What is the most important thing money can do for you?*
You: _____
_____
_____

Your spouse: _____
_____
_____

207. *Do you feel you had enough education? If you could go back to school, what would you study?*
You: _____
_____
_____

Your spouse: _____
_____
_____

208. If you were in trouble, who would you go to for advice?
You: _____
_____
_____
_____

Your spouse: _____
_____
_____
_____

209. What was your biggest obstacle in life, how did you overcome it?
You: _____
_____
_____
_____

Your spouse: _____
_____
_____
_____

210. Who was the first person in your life who died and how did you feel?
You: _____
_____
_____
_____

Your spouse: _____
_____
_____
_____

211. What was your favorite age so far?
    You: _____
    _____
    _____
    _____

    Your spouse: _____
    _____
    _____
    _____

212. Do you think men love differently than women?
    You: _____
    _____
    _____
    _____

    Your spouse: _____
    _____
    _____
    _____

213. What did you think about my parents the first time you met them?
    You: _____
    _____
    _____
    _____

    Your spouse: _____
    _____
    _____
    _____

214. Who has influenced your life the most?
    You: _____
    _____
    _____
    _____

    Your spouse: _____
    _____
    _____
    _____

215. Are you a positive or negative person?
    You: _____
    _____
    _____
    _____

    Your spouse: _____
    _____
    _____
    _____

216. How much sleep do you need?
    You: _____
    _____
    _____
    _____

    Your spouse: _____
    _____
    _____
    _____

217. *If you could wake up tomorrow in someone else's body, whose would you pick?*
    You: _____

    Your spouse: _____

218. *In what ways will you treat your children differently than how you were treated?*
    You: _____

    Your spouse: _____

219. *Would you point out a noticeable self destructive behavior in someone to them?*
    You: _____

    Your spouse: _____

220. What things are too personal to discuss with others?
You: _____
_____
_____

Your spouse: _____
_____
_____

221. What do you like best about your life?
You: _____
_____
_____

Your spouse: _____
_____
_____

222. What do you like least about your life?
You: _____
_____
_____

Your spouse: _____
_____
_____

223. *Do you do what you say you will do?*
    You: _____
    _____
    _____

    Your spouse: _____
    _____
    _____

224. *What does it take for you to trust someone?*
    You: _____
    _____
    _____

    Your spouse: _____
    _____
    _____

225. *What are you never willing to sacrifice?*
    You: _____
    _____
    _____

    Your spouse: _____
    _____
    _____

226. Would you murder someone to be able to end world hunger?
You: _____
_____
_____
_____

Your spouse: _____
_____
_____
_____

227. What has been your biggest disappointment in life?
You: _____
_____
_____
_____

Your spouse: _____
_____
_____
_____

228. Do you tend to talk more or listen more in conversations?
You: _____
_____
_____
_____

Your spouse: _____
_____
_____
_____

229. *How much do you like your body?*
You: _____

Your spouse: _____

230. *What did you learn as a child that has been most valuable to you in your life?*
You: _____

Your spouse: _____

231. *Have you ever regretted yelling at someone?*
You: _____

Your spouse: _____

232. *Have you ever stolen anything?*
You: _____
_____
_____

Your spouse: _____
_____
_____

233. *If you had one day left to live what would you do?*
You: _____
_____
_____

Your spouse: _____
_____
_____

234. *Tell me what would make someone a best friend?*
You: _____
_____
_____

Your spouse: _____
_____
_____

235. What would make them the worst friend?
    You: _____

    Your spouse: _____

236. What is the best decision you ever made?
    You: _____

    Your spouse: _____

237. Would you rather stay where we are or move to another city?
    You: _____

    Your spouse: _____

238. Would you rather 1 million dollars or 10 more years of life?
You: _____
_____
_____
_____

Your spouse: _____
_____
_____
_____

239. What's your favorite date that we've gone on together?
You: _____
_____
_____
_____

Your spouse: _____
_____
_____
_____

240. When do you feel most loved?
You: _____
_____
_____
_____

Your spouse: _____
_____
_____
_____

241. *What do you wish we did more of as a couple/family?*
You: _____
_____
_____

Your spouse: _____
_____
_____

242. *What do you wish we did less of as a couple/family?*
You: _____
_____
_____

Your spouse: _____
_____
_____

243. *Who do you think models good parenting?*
You: _____
_____
_____

Your spouse: _____
_____
_____

244. *What parts of our life could we use more adventure?*
You: _____
_____
_____

Your spouse: _____
_____
_____

245. *What are some ways could better use our time, talent, and finances?*
You: _____
_____
_____

Your spouse: _____
_____
_____

246. *How have you felt hopeful lately?*
You: _____
_____
_____

Your spouse: _____
_____
_____

247. If our love story was written, what would the title be?
    You: _____
    _____
    _____
    _____

    Your spouse: _____
    _____
    _____
    _____

248. What have you learned to like about me that you didn't know I had when we married?
    You: _____
    _____
    _____
    _____

    Your spouse: _____
    _____
    _____
    _____

249. Is our home as spiritual/religious as you'd like it to be?
    You: _____
    _____
    _____
    _____

    Your spouse: _____
    _____
    _____
    _____

250. If you could live one day over and over again for the rest of your life, what would it be?

You: _____

Your spouse: _____

251. What are you ok going into debt for?

You: _____

Your spouse: _____

252. What is your favorite memory of our wedding day?

You: _____

Your spouse: _____

253. When do you feel respected by me?
    You: _____
    _____
    _____

    Your spouse: _____
    _____
    _____

254. What is one thing you never want me to change about myself?
    You: _____
    _____
    _____

    Your spouse: _____
    _____
    _____

255. What is one thing I do that you appreciate the most?
    You: _____
    _____
    _____

    Your spouse: _____
    _____
    _____

256. Would you prefer to own your own business or work for someone else?
You: _____
_____
_____
_____

Your spouse: _____
_____
_____
_____

257. How would you feel if my job required that we travel a lot for work?
You: _____
_____
_____
_____

Your spouse: _____
_____
_____
_____

258. What keeps you going everyday?
You: _____
_____
_____

Your spouse: _____
_____
_____
_____

259. Are we happy with how household chores are divided up in our house?

You: _____

Your spouse: _____

260. Our kids would be shocked if we...

You: _____

Your spouse: _____

261. What is one thing you wish we had done before the kids but haven't?

You: _____

Your spouse: _____

262. I laugh so hard when you...
You: _____
_____
_____
_____

Your spouse: _____
_____
_____
_____

263. Our marriage works really well because...
You: _____
_____
_____
_____

Your spouse: _____
_____
_____
_____

264. What has changed about me since we got married?
You: _____
_____
_____
_____

Your spouse: _____
_____
_____
_____

265. *What did you expect your life to be at this age? How is it different than what you thought?*
You: _____
_____
_____

Your spouse: _____
_____
_____

266. *What do you worry about failing at?*
You: _____
_____
_____

Your spouse: _____
_____
_____

267. *What are you most proud of about us?*
You: _____
_____
_____

Your spouse: _____
_____
_____

268. What are 3 things you need to hear me say more often?
You: _____
_____
_____
_____

Your spouse: _____
_____
_____
_____

269. What item of clothing do you really like to see me wearing?
You: _____
_____
_____
_____

Your spouse: _____
_____
_____
_____

270. What did your grandparents house look like?
You: _____
_____
_____
_____

Your spouse: _____
_____
_____
_____

271. What were you not allowed to own or play with as a child?
You: _____

Your spouse: _____

272. Have you ever lost something or someone you truly loved?
You: _____

Your spouse: _____

273. Do you prefer careful planning or spontaneity?
You: _____

Your spouse: _____

274. How important are birthdays and anniversaries in your opinion?
You: _____
_____
_____
_____

Your spouse: _____
_____
_____
_____

275. Which household chores do you like to do the most?
You: _____
_____
_____
_____

Your spouse: _____
_____
_____
_____

276. What made you accept when I asked you out on a date?
You: _____
_____
_____
_____

Your spouse: _____
_____
_____
_____

277. What do you wish you could spend more of your time doing?
You: _____

Your spouse: _____

278. Worst advice you ever received?
You: _____

Your spouse: _____

279. What bad thing happened to you that actually turned out for the best?
You: _____

Your spouse: _____

280. What compliment would you really like to hear from me?
You: _____
_____
_____

Your spouse: _____
_____
_____

281. What are some things I do now that you couldn't live without?
You: _____
_____
_____

Your spouse: _____
_____
_____

282. What scares you about getting older?
You: _____
_____
_____

Your spouse: _____
_____
_____

283. *Does change excite or scare you?*
You: _____
_____
_____
_____

Your spouse: _____
_____
_____
_____

284. *What's one thing about your parents marriage that you admire?*
You: _____
_____
_____
_____

Your spouse: _____
_____
_____
_____

285. *What do you consider my greatest attribute?*
You: _____
_____
_____
_____

Your spouse: _____
_____
_____
_____

286. What is your favorite type of romantic gesture?
You: _____
_____
_____

Your spouse: _____
_____
_____

287. How do you think we should show appreciation to each other?
You: _____
_____
_____

Your spouse: _____
_____
_____

288. When have you felt the most loved by me?
You: _____
_____
_____

Your spouse: _____
_____
_____

289. *What's your favorite way I touch you?*
You: _____
_____
_____
_____

Your spouse: _____
_____
_____
_____

290. *What do you love most about me?*
You: _____
_____
_____
_____

Your spouse: _____
_____
_____
_____

291. *What were you thinking about the first time you saw me?*
You: _____
_____
_____
_____

Your spouse: _____
_____
_____
_____

292. What do you remember about our first kiss?
    You: _____
    _____
    _____
    _____

    Your spouse: _____
    _____
    _____
    _____

293. Why did you think I was good husband/wife material?
    You: _____
    _____
    _____
    _____

    Your spouse: _____
    _____
    _____
    _____

294. What made you the most excited about getting married?
    You: _____
    _____
    _____
    _____

    Your spouse: _____
    _____
    _____
    _____

295. *What's the best part of how we met?*
    You: _____
    _____
    _____
    _____

    Your spouse: _____
    _____
    _____
    _____

Next section

Relationship Questions
Hardest level of intensity

This section of questioning is a bit more challenging than the previous sections. That's due to deeper nature of the questions and more of a look into the highs and lows of your relationship.

Breathe and do your best not to get reactive, even if you don't like the answer that your spouse is sharing.

It's not so much a criticism of you, but a window into the world of your spouse and what it's like to be him/her.

Remember, you're a traveling guest and you want to be invited back to the country of your spouse, even if you don't understand the language spoken there.

Do what you need to do to protect yourself and make yourself feel safe and keep going once you've taken those steps.

1. *What is your greatest hope for our marriage?*
   You: _____
   _____
   _____
   _____

   Your spouse: _____
   _____
   _____
   _____

2. *What is your greatest hope for our children?*
   You: _____
   _____
   _____
   _____

   Your spouse: _____
   _____
   _____
   _____

3. *What do you consider your greatest strength?*
   You: _____
   _____
   _____
   _____

   Your spouse: _____
   _____
   _____
   _____

4. *What do you consider my greatest strength?*
   You: _____
   _____
   _____

   Your spouse: _____
   _____
   _____

5. *What do you consider your greatest weakness?*
   You: _____
   _____
   _____

   Your spouse: _____
   _____
   _____

6. *What do you consider my greatest weakness?*
   You: _____
   _____
   _____

   Your spouse: _____
   _____
   _____

7. *What memory would you like to make together?*
   You: _____
   _____
   _____

   Your spouse: _____
   _____
   _____

8. *What was the most important thing you learned from your parents?*
   You: _____
   _____
   _____

   Your spouse: _____
   _____
   _____

9. *What are 3 things you love about me?*
   You: _____
   _____
   _____

   Your spouse: _____
   _____
   _____

10. What was your most traumatic experience?
    You: _____
    _____
    _____
    _____

    Your spouse: _____
    _____
    _____
    _____

11. What do you hate most about yourself?
    You: _____
    _____
    _____
    _____

    Your spouse: _____
    _____
    _____
    _____

12. What words upset you the most?
    You: _____
    _____
    _____
    _____

    Your spouse: _____
    _____
    _____
    _____

13. *What is the worst thing someone ever said to you?*
    You: _____
    _____
    _____

    Your spouse: _____
    _____
    _____

14. *What is an internal conflict you have?*
    You: _____
    _____
    _____

    Your spouse: _____
    _____
    _____

15. *What is your most embarrassing moment?*
    You: _____
    _____
    _____

    Your spouse: _____
    _____
    _____

16. *Favorite thing about yourself?*
    You: _____
    _____
    _____

    Your spouse: _____
    _____
    _____

17. *What are you really good at?*
    You: _____
    _____
    _____

    Your spouse: _____
    _____
    _____

18. *What was the reason for your last break up?*
    You: _____
    _____
    _____

    Your spouse: _____
    _____
    _____

19. *Who is someone you miss?*
    You: _____
    _____
    _____

    Your spouse: _____
    _____
    _____

20. *What is your description of your best friend?*
    You: _____
    _____
    _____

    Your spouse: _____
    _____
    _____

21. *How often do you set goals for yourself?*
    You: _____
    _____
    _____

    Your spouse: _____
    _____
    _____

22. *When have you given up on something?*
    You: _____
    _____
    _____
    _____

    Your spouse: _____
    _____
    _____
    _____

23. *Where do you find purpose in your life?*
    You: _____
    _____
    _____
    _____

    Your spouse: _____
    _____
    _____
    _____

24. *Who do you consider as family?*
    You: _____
    _____
    _____
    _____

    Your spouse: _____
    _____
    _____
    _____

25. *What role does family play in your life?*
    You: _____

    Your spouse: _____

26. *Why do people do things which they know are bad?*
    You: _____

    Your spouse: _____

27. *What is the biggest sign of weakness in a person?*
    You: _____

    Your spouse: _____

28. *I really wish...*
    You: _____
    _____
    _____

    Your spouse: _____
    _____
    _____

29. *At what point are we good enough? When are we improved enough to accept ourselves?*
    You: _____
    _____
    _____

    Your spouse: _____
    _____
    _____

30. *What is one thing no one knows about you?*
    You: _____
    _____
    _____

    Your spouse: _____
    _____
    _____

31. When all is said and done, what do you want to be known or remembered for?

You: _____

Your spouse: _____

32. What is a quality you admire in others?

You: _____

Your spouse: _____

33. What are you afraid people see when they look at you?

You: _____

Your spouse: _____

34. What is the happiest you've ever felt?
You: _____
_____
_____
_____

Your spouse: _____
_____
_____
_____

35. What is the saddest you've ever felt?
You: _____
_____
_____
_____

Your spouse: _____
_____
_____
_____

36. Where do you feel the safest?
You: _____
_____
_____
_____

Your spouse: _____
_____
_____
_____

37. *What is one thing you want to overcome?*
    You: _____
    _____
    _____

    Your spouse: _____
    _____
    _____

38. *Describe yourself in one word?*
    You: _____
    _____
    _____

    Your spouse: _____
    _____
    _____

39. *What do you think the secret to a good life is?*
    You: _____
    _____
    _____

    Your spouse: _____
    _____
    _____

40. *What do you consider a wasted life?*
    You: _____
    _____
    _____
    _____

    Your spouse: _____
    _____
    _____
    _____

41. *What simple change could you make in your life that would have the biggest positive impact?*
    You: _____
    _____
    _____
    _____

    Your spouse: _____
    _____
    _____
    _____

42. *What is the biggest lie you've ever told?*
    You: _____
    _____
    _____
    _____

    Your spouse: _____
    _____
    _____
    _____

43. *What lesson in life did you have to learn the hard way?*
　　You: _____
　　_____
　　_____
　　_____

　　Your spouse: _____
　　_____
　　_____
　　_____

44. *What do you need to get off your chest?*
　　You: _____
　　_____
　　_____
　　_____

　　Your spouse: _____
　　_____
　　_____
　　_____

45. *When do you feel most loved by me?*
　　You: _____
　　_____
　　_____
　　_____

　　Your spouse: _____
　　_____
　　_____
　　_____

46. When is your spouse at his/her best?
    You: _____
    _____
    _____
    _____

    Your spouse: _____
    _____
    _____
    _____

47. What are you most grateful for in life?
    You: _____
    _____
    _____
    _____

    Your spouse: _____
    _____
    _____
    _____

48. If you could change one thing about how you were raised, what would you change?
    You: _____
    _____
    _____
    _____

    Your spouse: _____
    _____
    _____
    _____

49. Take 4 minutes and tell your spouse your life story in as much detail as possible?
   You: _____
   _____
   _____
   _____

   Your spouse: _____
   _____
   _____
   _____

50. What is too serious to be joked about?
   You: _____
   _____
   _____
   _____

   Your spouse: _____
   _____
   _____
   _____

51. What would you regret not having told someone if you weren't able to communicate with anyone after tonight. Why haven't you told them yet?
   You: _____
   _____
   _____
   _____

   Your spouse: _____
   _____
   _____
   _____

52. If your house suddenly was in a fire and you could only run back to save one item, what would it be? Why?

You: _____

_____

_____

_____

Your spouse: _____

_____

_____

_____

53. Share a personal problem and ask your spouse's advice on how he/she might handle it.

You: _____

_____

_____

_____

Your spouse: _____

_____

_____

_____

54. What is one thing that you need from me as a spouse that I am not giving you?

You: _____

_____

_____

_____

Your spouse: _____

_____

_____

_____

55. *What is one thing that I do that hurts you?*
    You: _____
    _____
    _____

    Your spouse: _____
    _____
    _____

56. *What is one thing I used to do that you still wish I did?*
    You: _____
    _____
    _____

    Your spouse: _____
    _____
    _____

57. *Are you ever jealous of something about me?*
    You: _____
    _____
    _____

    Your spouse: _____
    _____
    _____

58. *What do I do that you wish I would do less of?*
    You: _____
    _____
    _____
    _____

    Your spouse: _____
    _____
    _____
    _____

59. *Is our marriage different than you expected? In what ways?*
    You: _____
    _____
    _____
    _____

    Your spouse: _____
    _____
    _____
    _____

60. *What do you admire most about me?*
    You: _____
    _____
    _____
    _____

    Your spouse: _____
    _____
    _____
    _____

61. *What is one way I can support you more?*
    You: _____
    _____
    _____
    _____

    Your spouse: _____
    _____
    _____
    _____

62. *When do you feel least supported by me?*
    You: _____
    _____
    _____
    _____

    Your spouse: _____
    _____
    _____
    _____

63. *When do you feel most supported by me?*
    You: _____
    _____
    _____
    _____

    Your spouse: _____
    _____
    _____
    _____

64. *I don't like it when you say...*
    You: _____
    _____
    _____
    _____

    Your spouse: _____
    _____
    _____
    _____

65. *We've drifted apart because...*
    You: _____
    _____
    _____
    _____

    Your spouse: _____
    _____
    _____
    _____

66. *When this happened, I decided to do x and I see that has affected us...*
    You: _____
    _____
    _____
    _____

    Your spouse: _____
    _____
    _____
    _____

67. Has our relationship had any effect on your spirituality? How has it changed since we've been together?
You: _____

Your spouse: _____

68. Do you worry about our relationship? What would make you feel more secure?
You: _____

Your spouse: _____

69. Where do you see us in 5-10 years?
You: _____

Your spouse: _____

70. What do you wish for our relationship?
    You: _____
    _____
    _____
    _____

    Your spouse: _____
    _____
    _____
    _____

71. What do I do that annoys you?
    You: _____
    _____
    _____
    _____

    Your spouse: _____
    _____
    _____
    _____

72. Why do you think we've been put here on earth?
    You: _____
    _____
    _____
    _____

    Your spouse: _____
    _____
    _____
    _____

73. *Have I ever embarrassed you?*
    You: _____

    _____

    _____

    Your spouse: _____

    _____

    _____

74. *How do you know when I am happy?*
    You: _____

    _____

    _____

    Your spouse: _____

    _____

    _____

75. *How do you know when I am angry?*
    You: _____

    _____

    _____

    Your spouse: _____

    _____

    _____

76. *What upsets you most about our relationship?*
    You: _____
    _____
    _____
    _____

    Your spouse: _____
    _____
    _____
    _____

77. *What are you happiest about in our relationship?*
    You: _____
    _____
    _____
    _____

    Your spouse: _____
    _____
    _____
    _____

78. *Do you have any needs that are not being met? Is there something I can do to meet those needs?*
    You: _____
    _____
    _____
    _____

    Your spouse: _____
    _____
    _____
    _____

79. When you talk to others about me what do you say?
    You: _____
    _____
    _____

    Your spouse: _____
    _____
    _____

80. Does your family have any secrets they still won't talk about?
    You: _____
    _____
    _____

    Your spouse: _____
    _____
    _____

81. When did you first realize you loved me?
    You: _____
    _____
    _____

    Your spouse: _____
    _____
    _____

82. *Is it ok to keep a secret and why?*
    You: _____
    _____
    _____
    _____

    Your spouse: _____
    _____
    _____
    _____

83. *Who do you believe is the dominant one in our relationship?*
    You: _____
    _____
    _____
    _____

    Your spouse: _____
    _____
    _____
    _____

84. *How do you think love should be shown?*
    You: _____
    _____
    _____
    _____

    Your spouse: _____
    _____
    _____
    _____

85. *How much time do you think couples should spend together?*
    You: _____
    _____
    _____

    Your spouse: _____
    _____
    _____

86. *What do you enjoy doing with me?*
    You: _____
    _____
    _____

    Your spouse: _____
    _____
    _____

87. *What makes you feel insecure about life?*
    You: _____
    _____
    _____

    Your spouse: _____
    _____
    _____

88. What are your biggest struggles in life?
    You: _____
    _____
    _____
    _____

    Your spouse: _____
    _____
    _____
    _____

89. How much control do you feel you have over life?
    You: _____
    _____
    _____
    _____

    Your spouse: _____
    _____
    _____
    _____

90. Have you ever considered suicide? What would make life not worth living?
    You: _____
    _____
    _____

    Your spouse: _____
    _____
    _____
    _____

91. If you could find out what friends and acquaintances really think about you, would you want to know?

You: _____

_____

_____

Your spouse: _____

_____

_____

92. How much time and energy do you spend trying to impress other people?

You: _____

_____

_____

Your spouse: _____

_____

_____

93. What would make you feel betrayed?

You: _____

_____

_____

Your spouse: _____

_____

_____

94. *What is one thing you wish I did differently as a parent?*
    You: _____
    _____
    _____
    _____

    Your spouse: _____
    _____
    _____
    _____

95. *What is the hardest thing we've faced as a couple. How did we overcome it?*
    You: _____
    _____
    _____
    _____

    Your spouse: _____
    _____
    _____
    _____

96. *What miracles have happened for us?*
    You: _____
    _____
    _____
    _____

    Your spouse: _____
    _____
    _____
    _____

97. *When do you feel most emotionally connected to me?*
You: _____
_____
_____

Your spouse: _____
_____
_____

98. *Have you felt rejected by me? When?*
You: _____
_____
_____

Your spouse: _____
_____
_____

99. *Have you resented me? When?*
You: _____
_____
_____

Your spouse: _____
_____
_____

100. *What have we argued the most about recently?*
    You: _____

    Your spouse: _____

101. *What is one thing about our relationship that you wish you had the answer to?*
    You: _____

    Your spouse: _____

102. *What are the highest and lowest points of our relationship?*
    You: _____

    Your spouse: _____

103. *How can we affair proof our marriage?*
    You: _____
    _____
    _____

    Your spouse: _____
    _____
    _____

104. *How can we communicate better?*
    You: _____
    _____
    _____

    Your spouse: _____
    _____
    _____

105. *How can we trust each other better?*
    You: _____
    _____
    _____

    Your spouse: _____
    _____
    _____

106. *What do you want the atmosphere in our home to feel like?*
    You: _____
    _____
    _____
    _____

    Your spouse: _____
    _____
    _____
    _____

107. *What does your ideal life look like?*
    You: _____
    _____
    _____
    _____

    Your spouse: _____
    _____
    _____
    _____

108. *What brings you the most joy in our marriage?*
    You: _____
    _____
    _____
    _____

    Your spouse: _____
    _____
    _____
    _____

109. What are you dreading in life right now?
You: _____
_____
_____
_____

Your spouse: _____
_____
_____
_____

110. How do you feel the most connected with me?
You: _____
_____
_____
_____

Your spouse: _____
_____
_____
_____

111. What makes you feel most heard and understood when we communicate?
You: _____
_____
_____
_____

Your spouse: _____
_____
_____
_____

112. *What do you think we need to work on the most?*
 You: _____
 _____
 _____

 Your spouse: _____
 _____
 _____

113. *Do you believe that I love you?*
 You: _____
 _____
 _____

 Your spouse: _____
 _____
 _____

114. *What is the best advice you ever got?*
 You: _____
 _____
 _____

 Your spouse: _____
 _____
 _____

115. *When do you think it is okay to lie?*
    You: _____
    _____
    _____

    Your spouse: _____
    _____
    _____

116. *Did you ever dislike me when we first met?*
    You: _____
    _____
    _____

    Your spouse: _____
    _____
    _____

117. *How do you define emotional and physical infidelity?*
    You: _____
    _____
    _____

    Your spouse: _____
    _____
    _____

118. How much influence do you feel our family should have on our marriage?
    You: _____
    _____
    _____
    _____

    Your spouse: _____
    _____
    _____
    _____

119. How can I show you that I love you?
    You: _____
    _____
    _____
    _____

    Your spouse: _____
    _____
    _____
    _____

120. What is something I could do that would make you not trust me?
    You: _____
    _____
    _____
    _____

    Your spouse: _____
    _____
    _____
    _____

121. *Are there any rules you want to establish for our marriage?*
 You: _____
 _____
 _____

 Your spouse: _____
 _____
 _____

122. *Are there changes you'd like me to make so I can enjoy life more?*
 You: _____
 _____
 _____

 Your spouse: _____
 _____
 _____

123. *My greatest need right now as a man is...*
 You: _____
 _____
 _____

 Your spouse: _____
 _____
 _____

124. *My greatest need right now as a woman is...*
    You: _____
    _____
    _____
    _____

    Your spouse: _____
    _____
    _____
    _____

125. *How can I help you when you are angry?*
    You: _____
    _____
    _____
    _____

    Your spouse: _____
    _____
    _____
    _____

126. *What is your favorite way to show affection?*
    You: _____
    _____
    _____
    _____

    Your spouse: _____
    _____
    _____
    _____

127. *What is your favorite way to receive affection?*
    You: _____
    _____
    _____
    _____

    Your spouse: _____
    _____
    _____
    _____

128. *What should we do if we can't agree on something big?*
    You: _____
    _____
    _____
    _____

    Your spouse: _____
    _____
    _____
    _____

129. *Is there something you feel like is missing in your life?*
    You: _____
    _____
    _____
    _____

    Your spouse: _____
    _____
    _____
    _____

130. One thing I love most about you is?
    You: _____
    _____
    _____
    _____

    Your spouse: _____
    _____
    _____
    _____

131. One thing you love most about me is?
    You: _____
    _____
    _____
    _____

    Your spouse: _____
    _____
    _____
    _____

132. What are some ways you feel heard?
    You: _____
    _____
    _____
    _____

    Your spouse: _____
    _____
    _____
    _____

133. *I wish we could do... again*
You: _____
_____
_____

Your spouse: _____
_____
_____

134. *I love it when you...*
You: _____
_____
_____

Your spouse: _____
_____
_____

135. *I hate it when you...*
You: _____
_____
_____

Your spouse: _____
_____
_____

136. *Is there anything I need to apologize for that hurt you?*
 You: _____
 _____
 _____
 _____

 Your spouse: _____
 _____
 _____
 _____

137. *How would you best feel pursued by me?*
 You: _____
 _____
 _____
 _____

 Your spouse: _____
 _____
 _____
 _____

138. *What's the best way I can show you that you are my priority?*
 You: _____
 _____
 _____
 _____

 Your spouse: _____
 _____
 _____
 _____

139. *What burdens are you carrying that we can manage together?*
    You: _____
    _____
    _____
    _____

    Your spouse: _____
    _____
    _____
    _____

140. *Did I show you enough appreciation this week?*
    You: _____
    _____
    _____
    _____

    Your spouse: _____
    _____
    _____
    _____

141. *What is something I did that made you feel loved this week?*
    You: _____
    _____
    _____
    _____

    Your spouse: _____
    _____
    _____
    _____

142. *Is cheating ever okay?*
    You: _____
    _____
    _____
    _____

    Your spouse: _____
    _____
    _____
    _____

Next section

Intimacy Questions

We've included a set of relationship questions having to do with the bedroom. We've separated these questions out of the easy, medium, and harder line of questioning in case you are listening to this audio with others and you may feel uncomfortable in their presence. These questions aren't rated by intensity level- just bundled all into one section on sex and intimacy.

1. *What makes you uncomfortable when talking about intimacy?*
   You: _____
   _____
   _____

   Your spouse: _____
   _____
   _____

2. *What helps you relax so you can be fully present?*
   You: _____
   _____
   _____

   Your spouse: _____
   _____
   _____

3. *What makes you most comfortable?*
   You: _____
   _____
   _____

   Your spouse: _____
   _____
   _____

4. What is the most awkward romantic encounter you've ever had?
   You: _____
   _____
   _____

   Your spouse: _____
   _____
   _____

5. When am I most attractive to you?
   You: _____
   _____
   _____

   Your spouse: _____
   _____
   _____

6. What is the ideal number to be intimate per week?
   You: _____
   _____
   _____

   Your spouse: _____
   _____
   _____

7. What would you change about our intimate life?
   You: _____
   _____
   _____

   Your spouse: _____
   _____
   _____

8. What parts of my body do you love the most?
   You: _____
   _____
   _____

   Your spouse: _____
   _____
   _____

9. How do I make you a better person?
   You: _____
   _____
   _____

   Your spouse: _____
   _____
   _____

10. *What makes you uncomfortable in the bedroom?*
    You: _____
    _____
    _____

    Your spouse: _____
    _____
    _____

11. *How do you feel after we are intimate?*
    You: _____
    _____
    _____

    Your spouse: _____
    _____
    _____

12. *Do you feel safe sexually with me?*
    You: _____
    _____
    _____

    Your spouse: _____
    _____
    _____

13. What do you need to do to get in the mood?
    You: _____
    _____
    _____
    _____

    Your spouse: _____
    _____
    _____
    _____

14. What are sexual and non sexual touches that you love the most and wish I would do more often?
    You: _____
    _____
    _____
    _____

    Your spouse: _____
    _____
    _____
    _____

15. Do you like hugging or kissing more?
    You: _____
    _____
    _____
    _____

    Your spouse: _____
    _____
    _____
    _____

16. *What do you like about our sex life?*
    You: _____
    _____
    _____

    Your spouse: _____
    _____
    _____

17. *What do you dislike about our sex life?*
    You: _____
    _____
    _____

    Your spouse: _____
    _____
    _____

18. *What is the most sensitive part of your body?*
    You: _____
    _____
    _____

    Your spouse: _____
    _____
    _____

19. *What's your favorite way I touch you?*
    You: _____
    _____
    _____
    _____

    Your spouse: _____
    _____
    _____
    _____

20. *When is your favorite time to be intimate?*
    You: _____
    _____
    _____
    _____

    Your spouse: _____
    _____
    _____
    _____

21. *What is your favorite type of kiss?*
    You: _____
    _____
    _____
    _____

    Your spouse: _____
    _____
    _____
    _____

22. *What do I do during the day that makes you excited to be together later in the evening?*
    You: _____
    _____
    _____
    _____

    Your spouse: _____
    _____
    _____
    _____

23. *I always love it when you...*
    You: _____
    _____
    _____
    _____

    Your spouse: _____
    _____
    _____
    _____

Caring behaviors, romantic gestures, date ideas, love language activities

You've learned a lot about each other. Now it is time to take action. While most couples would say that they show love and care for their spouse, sometimes the recipient just doesn't feel it.

Despite your valiant efforts, what many couples don't realize is that the way we show love to our spouse is not necessarily the way our spouse needs to feel loved.

I came across this discovery when working with a couple many years ago and see it reoccur time and again with the couples I counsel. The "mushy" husband loved to express his feelings for his wife repeatedly in our sessions. It was clear he was crazy about her and was devoted to her forever. That's why it was bizarre when she admitted that she didn't feel loved.

Her explanation was rather revealing. Words didn't do it for her. She liked when her husband bought her gifts, even chocolates. That is how she felt loved. She, herself, was not that expressive and hardly ever said, "I love you" to her husband. He also felt unloved, and she was surprised he did not notice all of the work she did around the house, taking care of the kids, and making meals. Those were her demonstrations of her love for her husband.

This was a monumental breakthrough. Couples could give and give but continue to miss the mark. They could feel unappreciated and resentful, and helpless about ever pleasing their spouse. If they could only speak to their spouse in their spouse's love language, their spouse would actually feel loved.

As I learned more about Dr Gary Chapman's *5 Love Languages*, I began to see how couples have opposite love languages. This connected with my belief that marriage is the ultimate growth opportunity. Instead of focusing on ourselves and what makes us feel loved, we need to focus on the other and what makes them feel loved. Learning to love the way our partner feels loved gives us an opportunity to grow into a more balanced person. So if you are not that verbally expressive, your spouse's need for words of affirmation will compel you to be more communicative of your feelings.

Here are the five love languages:

1. **Words of affirmation:** While everyone enjoys a good word, some of us need more affirmation than others. How often do you tell your husband you love and appreciate him? When was the last time you told your wife you liked her outfit or that she looked nice? For those who need words of affirmation, their absence can lead to feelings of resentment. While you may be thinking or feeling good thoughts about your spouse, try verbalizing them and see the power of your words.

2. **Quality time:** While you may be the type that feels connected to your spouse, even when you are thousands of miles away, many spouses need to go out on a date or take a vacation to feel valued. You may be working so hard to provide for the family that you don't even spend time with your spouse. Quality time with your spouse is a great way to show that they are a priority in your life.

3. **Receiving gifts:** If you are the type that doesn't need anything, it may be hard for you to give gifts. I remember when I was getting engaged and heard about all of the gifts I was expected to give, a bracelet, an engagement ring… Coming from a family of all boys, it was hard for me to appreciate why anyone would want jewelry but I realized the positive message of love and care that my soon-to-be wife would feel. Even if you wouldn't want someone to spend money on you, focus on the feeling that the receiver will have and give with a full heart.

4. **Acts of service:** As the wife in the story above, some of us show and feel loved through giving of ourselves. Whether it is washing the dishes, helping out with the kids, or driving carpool, when our spouse performs acts of service we may feel more loved than if we received even the kindest word or gift.

5. **Physical Touch:** Some people crave physical affection more than others to feel loved. I have had many couples whose key complaint was that their spouse was not physical enough. While giving a hug for no particular reason may have been difficult for their spouse, this was precisely what was needed for them to feel cared for. If

touch is the way to show your spouse your love, make an extra effort to initiate contact. A simple hug, kiss, or even touch on the arm can go a long way.

There are three main questions you can ask yourself to discover your love language. How do you most often express your love to others? If you are always doing community service, that may be a good hint to how you express your care for others.

What do you complain about most often? If you constantly tell your spouse that they never take you out anywhere, you probably need more quality time to feel loved.

What do you request most often? If you are asking for more hugs and kisses, physical touch is likely the language that speaks to you. While it is possible to have more than one love language, there is usually one that is primary.

Begin to learn how you and your spouse feel loved and put this into practice. You will be amazed how years of frustration can dramatically shift. Even if you are experiencing conflict, the breath of fresh air of speaking each other's love language will cut through a lot of the negativity and bring you to a better and more constructive place from which to work on your marriage. When you finally hit the mark, you will experience renewed love and appreciation for your spouse.

Write a list of everything your spouse has done for you in the past that made you feel loved or cared for, currently does, or you secretly wish they would do. After reviewing that list, look and see if there are any patterns. More often than not, you will see one or two primary themes. That is your love language.

If you do this exercise with your spouse, you can exchange lists and commit to performing two or three items every day. Obviously, these should be items that are doable on a regular basis. You wouldn't buy a diamond ring for your spouse every day, but you could stop at the store to buy a surprise treat. Your spouse can also extrapolate based on your love language and pick similar behaviors.

Remember, even if you don't feel like it or are upset with each other, make sure you are consistent and do these behaviors regardless. It will help break the ice and keep you connected even if you are having a momentary lapse.

If you are doing this exercise alone, understanding your love language will help you realize how you may show love and that it may differ from what your spouse needs. You can also think about what your spouse enjoys, even if he/she is not doing the exercise, and make an effort to show love in those ways. More often than not, you will have a different love language, so knowing yours can help you better guess your spouse's language.

This exercise is extremely powerful. As the saying goes, "talk is cheap." One can talk a good game, but the bottom line is action. When you begin to show each other by taking concrete steps to improve your relationship, you will strengthen both the trust and love.

We'll provide some ideas for you to get really specific about the caring behaviors that you commit to.

Our suggestions will be divided up according to love language so you can easily find your spouse's love language and give them what they need to truly feel loved!

Words of Affirmation: This love language is where your husband or wife need to hear your encouraging and uplifting words to boost their confidence. Letting him know how much you appreciate him, find her attractive are going to truly fill up their "bucket". Find creative ways to share 2 or 3 of these meaningful words per day, in-person, by way of a short video, or through a love note hidden in his lunchbox, or stuck to her mirror.

Spouse's who need words of affirmation are going to need to hear "I love you" often and be truly heard when they are sharing. These folks love praise and wouldn't mind an email, text, or call sent during the day just to let them know you're thinking of them.

Get creative with these! You might have to go out of your comfort zone a bit especially if you're not someone who is comfortable with words and the results will be well worth it. Have fun- write a poem, dedicate a song to them, make a play list, praise them on social media, leave a note under their windshield wipers, write them a card. Lots of positivity and compliments are going to knock their socks off!

Share 2 or 3 of these per day

1. "I appreciate you"

2. "You are the most _____ I've ever met"

3. "Thank you for being the most amazing _____"

4. "I admire how _____ you are"

5. "You are such a supportive person"

6. "I am so proud of you"

7. "I notice how _____ you are- even if you don't show it so often"

8. "I am so blessed to have met you"

9. "You are such a beautiful person"

10. "You bring out the best in me"

11. "I need you"

12. "I learn something from you every day"

13. "I want to spend the rest of my life with you"

14. "You know how much you mean to me, don't you"

15. "I feel so happy when I'm with you"

16. "I love your smile"

17. "You make me laugh when I need it!"

18. "I can always be myself with you"

19. "I am so lucky to know you"

20. "Thank you for opening up with me"

21. "You are the best"

22. "I love your (physical attributes)"

23. "I trust you"

24. "You are such an amazing partner"

25. "You make my heart feel full"

26. "I want to do things for you everyday"

27. "You are such a strong person"

28. "I want you to have only the best"

29. "You are so loving"

30. "You make my life so meaningful"

31. "I think about you a lot"

32. "You always have the best ideas"

33. "I love spending time with you"

34. "You look amazing"

35. "You are perfect to me"

36. "You're so beautiful"

37. "You're so attractive"

38. "You're so smart"

39. "I trust your judgment"

40. "I respect you"

41. "I care about how you feel"

42. "You are such a hard worker"

43. "I am so blessed to have met you"

44. "You are such a beautiful person"

45. "I want and will care for you always"

46. "You mean so much to me"

47. "I have never met a person as good as you"

48. "Thank you for being so _____"

49. "I love spending time with you"

50. "I can't imagine life without you"

51. "I love you"

52. "There's no one else I'd rather be with right now"

53. "You are my best friend"

54. "You matter"

55. "You are so strong"

56. "You look so handsome"

57. "You are gorgeous"

58. "You are a dream come true"

Quality Time: This spouse is going to need weekly date nights preferably. Or time during the day if you can swing a quick walk, picnic, a bath together, an unplanned car ride adventure.

You can even do the things you normally do- such as watching TV together, the game, a movie, or even bedtime, just this time- put your phone or Facebook away- so the time you are spending together is indeed quality.

Going to dinner or even eating dinner at home without your phones could hit the spot for this spouse as is going to bed at the same time.

These suggestions might not be that big of a deal for you, and if your love language isn't quality time, then it's not going to be what you need, and you'd be surprised just how meaningful it will be to your spouse.

More suggestions are anything that will give uninterrupted attention- talking about a book you've read, a movie watched- don't juggle other things while listening and conversing when you're being intentional about giving your spouse quality time.

Make a run to Starbucks together, take your lunch break together, bike riding, a class, run errands- just make the trip about each other. Plan, dream for your future together- remember, spending quality time together doesn't have to cost a lot of money, it's about focused, uninterrupted attention of your spouse that matters.

Receiving Gifts: Another love language that doesn't have to cost a lot of money (but can if you want it to!) is a pre-planned surprise/gift for your partner whose love language is gifts.

Sometimes just picking up lunch at work or having flowers on the table when they get home scores loads of points with your gift loving spouse.

Of course, remembering all holidays, birthdays, special occasions, and anniversaries is going to be important- perhaps with something homemade or even a storebought card you've written in.

Save up to buy something they may have casually mentioned wanting and give it with your whole heart. Going on a special date to their favorite place/restaurant and having a special gift waiting for them there- even a small token like a book or DVD you can watch together, a treat from the grocery store, pickup a favorite beer or dessert, pictures from a vacation or journal of special memories might excite them as much as an expensive gift!

If you can swing it - something like tickets to a favorite concert, a surprise vacation, or some friend time with the guys/girls - is going to be very fulfilling for a gift loving spouse.

Even if you're not someone who needs gifts or finds special occasions of importance, for a spouse whose love language is gifts, these dates are going to be very, very important and so celebrate them with as much fanfare as you can muster up!

Acts of Service: For a spouse whose love language is acts of service, you'll want to really think long and hard about all of the "burdens" and responsibilities that your spouse is taking on and find ways you can make their job easier.

Having coffee ready for them in the morning, emptying out the dishwasher, picking up their drycleaning, and cleaning their car might seem trivial to you- but for an acts of service needing spouse- will ease their troubles tremendously!

Their need to complete to-dos and chores can be endless and so shouldering the responsibility of chores like cleaning out the garage, handing them a warm towel after a shower, taking care of the kids and doing bedtime is going to really speak to them.

Watering the plants, changing the lightbulbs, running errands so they can have some time off is going to feel like you held up the world for them for a few hours!

Anything that makes him/her feel taken care of and pampered to some extent will be so comforting and loving in their mind. What could be better than that? Remember, in this case, actions speak louder than words.

Physical Touch: Of course, a spouse who loves and needs physical touch, is going to want as much intimacy as possible. Helping to fulfill his/her need for physical touch can also include non-sexual touches which may ease the pressure off you if you are not as sexual of a person.

Of course in marriages where there is any kind of past physical or sexual trauma, if one spouse's love language is indeed physical touch, there may be a large discrepancy or need there that requires some more intensive therapy to work out some of the feelings involved on both sides.

For now, this list of non sexual physical touch may help to ease some of the potential touchiness (no pun intended) of the subject.

Cuddling, hugging from behind, a back rub, holding hands, a foot rub, dancing, kisses, and sitting close is going to be wanted- not to forget about massage, tickles, and squeezing. Resting your head on a shoulder, touching a shoulder in passing, caressing an arm, touching foreheads can be romantic, and kissing when you first wake up can be romantic even for a spouse whose love language is not physical touch. Did we mention back scratching :)?

A High Energy Fun Bucket List of Adventures

Even adults needs to have fun. All because you are a responsible adult, doesn't mean that you can't have fun. In fact, fun is a necessary ingredient to keep your relationship vibrant and thriving. It's also something that can fall to the wayside with the busyness of life, work, and raising a family. That's why it is important to dedicate a section to help you make fun a regular part of your life. Fun helps shift the energy in a relationship. If things are feeling stale or tense, it is the quickest way to scramble the situation and pick things up. Before coming up with a game plan, it is worth reflecting on your beliefs about fun. Some of us carry baggage around fun. Perhaps every fun family outing was ruined by conflict. You may have received messages that fun is not ok. These are all important discussions to have together so you can see what may be getting in the way of you having fun in your relationship. Sometimes we have the opposite experience of our spouse and expect fun because it was a cherished part of our upbringing. That too is important to be aware of as we may have certain expectations entering the marriage. Learn about your feelings about fun and then begin to create a list of fun activities you can do together.

High energy fun is particularly what we are looking for. This is the kind of fun the gets your heart beating. While you may enjoy playing cards and it can bring about closeness, you'll get more bang for your buck if you do something a little more active. It need not be an organized sport. It can be something as easy as a belly laugh, a pillow fight, or jumping on the trampoline. The chemicals that are elicited from doing such activities together create the same bonding effect that occurs during intimacy. It's quite powerful for your relationship.

While it may seem totally counterintuitive to schedule fun, it is a must if you want to make sure it happens. Schedule a fun night, hire a standing babysitter, and enjoy your time together. It may just be the sanity you need each week, to keep you high level.

We'll give you some fun bucket list suggestions for activities you can do together.

These ideas will be separated according to budget so you know in advance what you can do on the cheap and what you need to invest more money into.

Not all suggestions are high energy so take your relationship temperature before deciding- if you're feeling distant from each other, choose an activity that is more likely to elicit a belly laugh. Just want some coziness? We've got you covered there too.

Fun Bucket List Ideas

- $
- ☐ Make cookies together
- ☐ Work on a painting together
- ☐ Sit down, dream and draft your 5 year plan together
- ☐ Lie out and watch the stars
- ☐ Have a movie marathon
- ☐ A spa night
- ☐ A photo shoot
- ☐ A water fight
- ☐ Play hide and seek
- ☐ Play basketball together
- ☐ Go skinny dipping
- ☐ Start a garden together
- ☐ Work on a DIY craft together
- ☐ Beer and wine tasting
- ☐ Drive in movie
- ☐ Build a blanket fort
- ☐ Attend a carnival
- ☐ Go antiquing
- ☐ Beach trip
- ☐ Watch the sunset
- ☐ Go camping
- ☐ Go on an unplanned road trip
- ☐ Karaoke night
- ☐ Bowling
- ☐ Personalized scavenger hunt
- ☐ Gun range
- ☐ Comedy show
- ☐ Take a brewery tour
- ☐ Take a DJing class

- ☐ Trapeze class
- ☐ Test drive expensive cars
- ☐ Make a relationship time capsule
- ☐ Play frisbee
- ☐ Fly kites
- ☐ Write a song/poem together
- ☐ Snowball fight
- ☐ Volunteer at a nursing home
- ☐ Decorate desserts together
- ☐ Attend a play
- ☐ Go to the circus
- ☐ Make lunches for the homeless
- ☐ Take a boxing class
- ☐ Watch the sunrise
- ☐ Show him where you grew up
- ☐ Go to an amusement park
- ☐ Make a bonfire
- ☐ Watch each other's favorite movies
- ☐ Play 20 questions
- ☐ Kiss in the rain
- ☐ Take a picture in a photo booth
- ☐ Go to a midnight movie
- ☐ Read the same book at the same time
- ☐ Write each other love letters
- ☐ Dress up in a couples costume for halloween
- ☐ Ride around town on a motorcycle
- ☐ Go ice skating
- ☐ Kiss on top of a ferris wheel
- ☐ Go for a hike
- ☐ Take a bubble bath
- ☐ Have breakfast in bed
- ☐ Recreate your first date

- ☐ Cover the bed in rose petals
- ☐ Cuddle by the fire
- ☐ Attend a film premiere
- ☐ Run a 5k together
- ☐ Take fun pictures in the rain
- ☐ Walk the beach at sunset
- ☐ Carve your initials in a tree
- ☐ Kiss underwater
- ☐ Late night swimming
- ☐ Car karaoke
- ☐ Water balloon fight
- ☐ Early morning run
- ☐ Video game date
- ☐ Go to a waterpark
- ☐ Tan in the sun
- ☐ Go sledding
- ☐ Throw a pool party
- ☐ Catch fireflies
- ☐ Go strawberry picking
- ☐ Bubblewrap each other
- ☐ Cooking contest
- ☐ Team eating contest
- ☐ Walk on the boardwalk
- ☐ Learn calligraphy
- ☐ Have a dance party
- ☐ Relax on a hammock
- ☐ Run through sprinklers
- ☐ Canoe ride
- ☐ Makeovers
- ☐ Beach yoga
- ☐ Fireworks show
- ☐ Paint pottery

- ☐ Finish a 1000 piece puzzle
- ☐ Go to a haunted house
- ☐ Build a snowman
- ☐ cornmaze
- ☐ Apple picking
- ☐ Make candy apples
- ☐ Carve pumpkins
- ☐ Enjoy a bookstore together
- ☐ Go to the local highschool football game
- ☐ Visit a local orchard
- ☐ Make food for the homeless
- ☐ Complete an obstacle race: tough mudder, zombie mud run
- ☐ Spend the entire day in bed
- ☐ Play Twister
- ☐ Mud wrestle
- ☐ Body paint each other
- ☐ Slow dance together to a romantic song
- ☐ Share a fear and get through it together
- ☐ Look at old pictures and reminisce
- ☐ Kiss at a red light
- ☐ Make a candlelight dinner
- ☐ Share inside jokes
- ☐ Go to a bar and dance

- **$$**
- ☐ Explore a new city
- ☐ Learn ballroom dancing
- ☐ Spa day and couples massage
- ☐ Concert
- ☐ Stay at a bed and breakfast
- ☐ Take a cooking class

- ☐ Trapeze class
- ☐ Paintballing, miniature golf
- ☐ Ride a tandem bicycle around your city
- ☐ Go backpacking through europe
- ☐ Go sailing
- ☐ Stay in an over water home
- ☐ Attend a gala
- ☐ Broadway show
- ☐ RV across the country

- **$$$$$**
- ☐ Horseback riding
- ☐ Hot air balloon ride
- ☐ Water skiing
- ☐ Go handgliding
- ☐ Plan a trip where you've never been
- ☐ Live in a different country
- ☐ Fly first class
- ☐ Rent a beach house for the summer
- ☐ Take a cruise
- ☐ Travel to all 7 continents
- ☐ Disneyworld
- ☐ Scuba diving
- ☐ Parasailing
- ☐ Design your own house and build it
- ☐ Float in the Dead Sea
- ☐ Stay in an ice hotel in Quebec
- ☐ See 24 hours of daylight in Alaska
- ☐ Visit an ancient city

Chapter 4

Relationship vision

You've made it to the final and most important section! Crafting your relationship vision- a mission statement for your couplehood together and in the future.

You know so much more now than you did about your partner before you started this journey together- of daily conversation, questioning, bucket list discussion, and communication about things both large and small.

You did it!

Realize that by answering some silly or serious questions, you've done more than many couples are able to in their lifetimes- communicating regularly, safely, without reacting- or driving a wedge further into the "illusion of separateness" rather than connecting.

You are two sides of the same coin- partners that you chose above everyone else.

Life can get scary at times, especially if you're struggling to keep the spark alive, and the Relationship Vision Couples

Reconnection Journal intends to help you get through those times of uncertainty.

You'll notice our questions were crafted carefully to never create more doubt about each other.

Sometimes other books or journals designed for couples ask questions that cause a couple to begin fighting more.

As relationship experts with an intensive marriage counseling practice, our priority is safety- and we feel it is NEVER prudent to cause a couple to doubt each other. This happens all too often in the world- even by well meaning friends, or social media comparisons to other couples, marriage therapists, and individual therapists- and we want to protect you from those unfortunate all to frequent phenomenons.

Take some time now to draft your joint relationship vision.

On two separate sheets of paper, both you and your spouse list your personal relationship vision. Entitle the page "My Relationship Vision." Write a positive, descriptive, and specific sentence. Instead of the negative, "we do not fight," put down the positive: "we get along together in a loving relationship." Vision has a magnetic power that draws people to it. As opposed to focusing on what we don't want and investing our energy in moving away from the past, away from the destruction, and mourning about what we no longer have or fear what could be, let us shift our attention to what we do want. This helps us move towards it with greater ease than getting stuck in our fears or our old way of being.

Formulate your vision in the present tense. As opposed to saying "we will be happy," write "we are happy." The future is here, now. Our dream relationship is before our eyes at this very moment. When we think of it this way, we can actually live it as opposed to waiting for it.

Once you have constructed your vision statements, using a separate line for each sentence, begin to rank the items according to relative value/importance to you by writing a number on the left column of the paper. On the right column rank items according to difficulty. Finally, circle the two most valuable items to your vision.

When you are both done, read each other your visions and note which items you have in common. Now, you are ready to create your shared relationship vision. On one piece of paper, write the title "Our Relationship Vision." Write down all of the mutually agreed upon items. Draw a line after the mutually agreed upon items and write down all of the other items that you had listed.

Once you are finished, post your relationship vision in a place where you will be able to see it. Take a moment every day to glance at it and/or spend a few minutes every week to read it together. Are your relationship choices and actions in line with that vision? Do you feel yourself moving towards that vision? Merely reading the vision on a regular basis can help create a shift in a relationship and move it in a positive direction. It will make you more conscious about what you really want. It also provides encouragement that you are making progress in achieving your vision.

For some couples, looking at the vision or reading it together is enough to keep it in the forefront of your mind. For others, it is helpful to have a further discussion about the items, explaining what you mean and how they could practically manifest themselves. You may even want to create an implementation plan so that you can take actual steps towards these goals.

Your vision is a work in progress. You can tweak it as you move along. The main thing is that you are charting a path together as you go on your relationship journey.

End Of Book

A preview of

The 5 Step Action Plan to a Happy & Healthy *Marriage*

Increase the Joy of Sanctity, Safety, and Stability in your Home

A GLOBAL INITIATIVE OF THE MARRIAGE RESTORATION PROJECT
KEEPING COUPLES TOGETHER, HAPPILY

Rabbi Shlomo Slatkin, MS, LCPC

The 5 Step Action Plan to a Happy & Healthy *Marriage*

Rabbi Shlomo Slatkin MS, LCPC

The 5 Step Action Plan to a Happy & Healthy *Marriage*

Increase the Joy of Sanctity, Safety, and Stability in your Home

©2011 - 2015 by
SHLOMO SLATKIN

All rights reserved. No part of this book may be reproduced in any form without permission in writing from the publisher, except in the case of brief quotations embodied in critical articles or reviews.

Cover & Interior Design: KDG Advertising - www.kdga.net
Photo Credit: Istock Imaging
www.TheMarriageRestorationProject.com

1 With this ring . . . A national survey on marriage in America. (2005). Gaithersburg, MD: The National Fatherhood Initiative

2 Stanley, S. M. (2005). The power of commitment: A guide to active lifelong love. San Francisco:Jossey-Bass

3 Covey, Steven (1989). The Seven Habits of Highly Effective People: Restoring the Character Ethic. Simon & Schuster Inc.

Author's Bio

Rabbi Shlomo Slatkin is a Licensed Clinical Professional Counselor, Certified Imago Relationship Therapist (Advanced Clinician), and an ordained Rabbi. He works with couples to empower them to develop a conscious and connected relationship through resolving conflict, learning communication skills, and rediscovering love. Rabbi Slatkin also uses this Imago couple therapy model with individuals, families, and organizations.

A gifted teacher who has lectured throughout the world, Rabbi Slatkin edited and co-authored the Jewish version of *Couplehood As a Spiritual Path*, a curriculum for synagogues based on Imago Relationship Therapy and Drs. Harville Hendrix and Helen LaKelly Hunt's *Getting The Love You Want*. He is also the author of *The Jewish Marriage Book: Improving Your Mar-*

riage One Jewish Holiday at a Time, as well as numerous published articles on relationships.

A graduate of Loyola University Maryland (formerly Loyola College), Rabbi Slatkin holds a master's degree in Counseling Psychology, with additional psychotherapy training at the Imago Relationship Institute. Rabbi Slatkin is a clinical member of the American Mental Health Counselors Association, Imago Relationships International, and the Mid-Atlantic Association of Imago Therapists.

THE 5 STEP ACTION PLAN TO A HAPPY & HEALTHY MARRIAGE

TABLE OF CONTENTS

Preface .... Pg 10

Introduction .... Pg 11

Action Step I - Commit ....Pg 21

Action Step II - Seal Your Exits ....Pg 47

Action Step III - Detox Your Marriage ....Pg 71

Action Step IV - Acknowledge the "Other"..Pg 83

Action Step V - Love Infusions ....Pg 120

Conclusion ....Pg 133

The 5 Step Action Plan Full Program...............Pg 138

The 2-Day Marriage Restoration Intensive ....Pg 140

Preface

With the divorce rate reaching epidemic proportions, *The Marriage Restoration Project* was created to uphold the institution of marriage and family by providing proven resources that make a difference. Much like a piece of priceless art can be restored after years of neglect, so too a marriage has the potential to be restored to its original connection.

It is all too easy to discard an old relationship that no longer seems to function. We hold the hope for every couple to be able to experience profound growth and healingin their relationship. *The Marriage Restoration Project* aims to restore even the most stagnant of relationships by restoring and reawakening the original, undying connection that exists between you and your partner.

Introduction

If you are reading this book, you are most likely experiencing marital crisis. Your life, as you know it, is under attack. You feel extremely unsafe and you don't know what to do. I have some good news for you. There is a way to protect yourself from the toxic energy that is destroying your relationship. In the following pages, you will learn a foolproof method for how to save your marriage, even if it is on the verge of destruction.

I remember about a year or so after 9/11 when there were warnings about the possibility of a chemical attack on the East Coast. My wife read up on how to protect us, ran to Home Depot, loaded up on supplies, and started sealing windows for a "safe room". We were terrified but felt a bit more capable of dealing with the threat after we took the necessary precautions. We learned that when dealing with any acute crisis, it is best to become informed and then decide what immediate action must be taken. We felt better having taken action.

The same applies to dealing with the crisis of your current relationship. You can point fingers and blame, you can come up with theories, and you can remain resentful, but if you do not take immediate action nothing will change and you'll continue to feel lousy.

WHAT SHOULD YOU DO?

Take action. *The 5 Step Action Plan to a Happy & Healthy Marriage* will present you with a tried and true action plan, guiding you every step of the way. The Plan is based on my years of training in Imago Relationship Therapy and working with couples, as well as my own personal life experience.

THE FIVE-STEPS ARE AS FOLLOWS:
ACTION STEP I- COMMIT
ACTION STEP II- SEAL YOUR EXITS
ACTION STEP III- DETOX YOUR MARRIAGE
ACTION STEP IV- ACKNOWLEDGE THE "OTHER"
ACTION STEP V- LOVE INFUSIONS

In Steps I and II, you will learn how to make your marriage a priority, refocus, and bring the energy back into your relationship. Step III will teach you how to remove counterproductive behaviors such as negativity that seek to undermine your connection and then you will be able to create more safety in your relationship. In Step IV, you will learn how to acknowledge the "other," learning new ways to connect so that understanding each other and feeling respected and listened to becomes your marriage's second nature. Finally, Step V will teach you how to bring back some of the spark you once felt in your relationship.

As with any plan, this is a step-by-step process. This means that ideally you need to follow the sequence to reach your intended goal. There are a few ways to go about this:

1) Read the book and stop to complete the exercises as you go along.

2) Read through the entire book one time without completing the exercises. Then read the book again, completing the exercises along the way.

Do I have to do the exercises?

Even if you choose option 2, you will inevitably have to do the exercises. The exercises are important because they will direct you in applying the material detailed in each action step to your personal situation. As you apply what you learn, you will bring about the desired change in your relationship. Otherwise, you will be reading about some interesting ideas that might stimulate your heart and your mind, inspiring you to see things differently, but in the end, you may lack the follow-through. The exercises will call you to act and therefore you can and will derive the maximum benefit from this book.

How long will it take?

It really depends on the amount of work you are willing to put in. Some action steps may be easier to apply than others. Let's take, for example, Action Step V: Love Infusions. A love infusion such as an appreciation or a caring behavior can be applied immediately. On the other hand, Action Step III: Detox Your Marriage can take considerably longer depending on your motivation to watch what you say.

You may even find yourself working on all steps simultaneously. Although the steps have a logical progression, you can still benefit by detoxing your marriage (Action Step III) even if you are struggling with commitment issues (Action Step I). So even though it is best to go in order, don't refrain from applying all of the action steps to whatever degree you can, as they all can enable the others to be fulfilled harmoniously.

Who should read this book?

The 5 Step Action Plan to a Happy & Healthy Marriage can be implemented by couples or individuals. In my experience, there is usually one spouse that is less enthusiastic about working on the relationship. While working together with your spouse is optimal and will be especially helpful if you wish to work on the Imago Dialogue (to be detailed in Action Step IV), you can read this book and implement all of the Five Action Steps even if you have an unwilling spouse. All of the Action Steps can be done on your own and you can improve your relationship even without your spouse being directly involved. The reason for that is that this program is not about changing what's wrong with your spouse but about taking personal responsibility for your relationship. If you work on yourself, those changes have a ripple effect on your relationship and your spouse will change.

RABBI SHLOMO SLATKIN

Change yourself, change your relationship: a story

When you change the way you "show up" in your relationship, you may notice that your spouse's resistance begins to wane and many of your complaints about your spouse disappear. One of my favorite examples is the wife who would constantly ask her husband to do things for her. She was often faced with resistance. When she would ask him something, he would not provide a straight answer. He was full of excuses. As she started taking more responsibility around the house cooking dinner, doing the laundry, jobs that her husband previously did something interesting happened. Not only was he happier, he was much more responsive.

He no longer found himself threatened or annoyed by her requests because he knew that by taking on the role of the homemaker, she had taken action to give him more space. What changed? She changed, and not because of his complaints or because she felt she had to. She changed from a place of health and wellbeing. After certain events triggered her to take a look at why she'd been avoiding doing basic homemaking tasks in the past, she became conscious about her feelings of resistance to being a homemaker. With that consciousness, she was able to make a decision that in the best interests of her family she needed to take more responsibility around the house. This change allowed her husband, always vigilant for fear of being taken advantage of, to relax.

The point of this story is that your relationship can improve by working on The Five-Step Action Plan, even without a willing spouse. Whether you read the book together with your spouse or go at it alone, I trust that you will find the The Five-Step Action Plan to be a user-friendly guide to achieving the relationship of your dreams!

Action Step I
Commit

Committing to the relationship

Commitment issues are not only relevant to premarital couples. In fact, studies show that the number one reason for divorce is not money or infidelity, though they're up there, but lack of commitment.[1] While you may have committed to getting married, you were in love. It was easy! Although you may have been told that marriage has its ups and downs, you were too blind to see reality at the time. "No, we will be different, we won't fight, and we have a good relationship." Now, five, ten, twenty years down the road, you realize how right they were. You weren't prepared for this, and when you pledged to love each other "for better or for worse," you did not commit to something this "worse." This means that if you want to save your marriage, it is time to commit, but this time it is with the full knowledge of what that entails.

What does it look like?

What does it mean to commit? Is it a decision, an attitude, an action? The good news is that if you are reading this book, it shows that you are already somewhat committed to your relationship; otherwise you wouldn't be interested in saving it. Commitment is a combination of all of the above. It requires a decision to be dedicated to the relationship, making it a priority in your life. That decision is followed by an attitude that your marriage comes first and you are willing to do what it takes to improve it. Finally, your actions for your marriage are the manifestation of your decision and your attitude. While the remaining Action Steps will focus on how to manifest your commitment in the world of action, Action Step One is making the decision to commit and developing an attitude of commitment.

Why Should I commit?

The couples that successfully get through crisis are the ones who are committed to their marriage. In our disposable society, a marriage is as expendable as a computer. You buy it knowing that you will have to replace it within a few years. A marriage is not a computer. It is a serious commitment that requires work and while it may seem much easier to leave the relationship, the truth is that it won't necessarily be so. The potential damage divorce does will make you think twice about throwing away your marriage.

Two forms of commitment

Let's examine some of the reasons why you should stay committed to your marriage. On a basic level, there are two forms of commitment- constraints and personal dedication.[2] Constraints are things that keep us in the relationship even if things are not going well. These include pressure from family and friends, financial concerns, children, negative beliefs about divorce, and fear of the future. While these constraints may be fear-based, they assist in keeping us from bolting when the going gets rough. However, these reasons are usually not enough in the long run.

What is needed for your relationship to endure is personal dedication, a real desire to be together with your spouse. It means making your relationship a priority and the willingness to sacrifice for the sake of the relationship. When this dedication is present, we feel safer and are more willing to give for the relationship to succeed. It helps us not get overwhelmed by the day-to-day challenges, as we have a long-term view of the marriage.

Do It for the Kids

If you are feeling lousy about your marriage, I imagine you may not necessarily feel like dedicating yourself to your relationship just yet. At the very least, though, you may have some constraints that may compel you to commit. The most compelling reason to think twice about calling it quits is your children. If you have a family, the damage that divorce can do to your children is exponential. Not only will it affect them when they get married but it will create pain and a host of mental health issues for them. Children of divorced parents are 50% more likely to get divorced themselves than children from unbroken homes. Divorce also doubles their risk of serious social, emotional, and psychological dysfunction. You may be unhappy in your marriage, but is it worth ruining the lives of your children as well?

While there is a common myth that your bad marriage, albeit intact, is worse for your kids in the long run, it just simply is not true. In spite of the fighting and unpleasantness, kids would much prefer to live in one world than have it split in two.

The collapse of the American family has destroyed our society. How many drug addicts, criminals, etc. grew up in a stable, two-parent household? Any guesses? When I worked in community mental health, I heard the saddest, most depressing stories of ruined lives that could have been so much better. Not one of those clients grew up in a two-parent household. When will we wake up and realize that many of our societal ills can be averted if we invest in fostering healthy relationships?

I cannot overemphasize the effect of an unstable home on your children. Many a time I will leave my office in the evening thinking about how so many of the couples I work with would not need my assistance if they did not have such traumatic childhoods. It is amazing the damage parents can do to their children. I see the effects on the next generation in their relationships and it is extremely upsetting. These are supposedly "normal" middle- to upper-middle-class families where the parents did not take ownership for their own emotional issues, which they probably inherited from their own parents. You have the unique opportunity to stop this "inheritance" and work on yourself so that you can provide a loving home that will nurture your children's emotional health. You may think divorce will solve the problem, but it won't. Take responsibility for your role in the marriage and work together with your spouse to create an environment where your children can thrive and develop into emotionally mature adults.

But what if I get remarried? Won't that provide my children with a stable home? Sorry to break it to you, but 65% of second marriages end in divorce. Second marriages with children are even more likely to be terminated. That means you run the risk of subjecting your children to another divorce. You are also making it more likely for your children to divorce later in life. Having a stepparent shows that spouses are expendable if they don't work out. Even if you stay married to your second spouse, there are still greater risk factors for children in stepfamilies.

Money, Money, Money

If you are still not convinced or you don't have children, let's see what happens to your finances when you divorce. A newspaper headline recently stated that couples are refraining from divorce as it is too expensive. The high financial cost of divorce has been verified time and time again by various divorce attorneys with whom I have spoken. One attorney I know actually discourages couples from getting divorced. Besides lawyer fees, whatever remains is usually split in half. This means you will have less than half the amount of money you currently have. Where as money issues can cause marriage problems, terminating your marriage may only make it worse.

No, you won't find someone better

As we see from the amount of divorces around us, these constraints were having less effect on keeping couples together. One major reason that you might be overlooking some of these realistic concerns is that you are convinced that your life could be better, especially if you are married to someone else. Maybe you married the wrong person. Despite the damage to your children and your finances, at least you could find someone else and live happily ever after. Well, I am sorry to burst your bubble, but this is a major fallacy. I have seen plenty of second marriages suffering from the same problems as were experienced in the first.

"Are You Sure I Won't Find Someone Better?"

Part of being committed to your marriage, or at least trying to make it work, is to realize that it is not all about the other person. What do YOU bring to the table? Why is it possible to get divorced and have problems with a second marriage? Is it purely coincidence, bad luck? While you leave your ex behind, you take yourself into whatever relationship you join.

A relationship takes two to tango and there is never one party that is entirely innocent. What responsibility do we take for our relationship disaster? Is our spouse simply an evil monster with "psychological" problems or do we play a role in triggering such undesirable behavior? As we will learn a bit later, most of the things that really bother us about our partner are only partially about them and largely about us. Why would a particular incident bother you tremendously but appear insignificant to your friend?

Each one of us has our own unique history as well as natural tendencies. Both shape who we are and determine how we process events and/or react to others. Our external triggers, as real as they may be, are only a symptom of a greater problem. That problem is our story and ourselves. By working on ourselves and becoming more conscious about why we react the way we do, we can learn how to be more effective in our relationships and have more compassion for our spouse.

Exercise Ia: Getting conscious about your triggers

Let's learn a little bit more about what bothers you so much about your spouse and why. Find a quiet place to sit down and either ponder or write down the answers to the following questions. If you have more than one annoyance, and you probably will, then you will want to answer the entire list of questions for each annoyance.

1) What annoys me about my spouse?
2) What hurts me so much about that?
3) What scares me about this?
4) How do I react?
5) What do I really need from my spouse?
6) What feels familiar about this experience?

****

Furthermore, these points of conflict are a blessing in disguise. Marriage is ultimately an opportunity for growth and healing. The challenges that we face are there to do just that, to challenge us to become better and more balanced people. The things that bother us most about our spouse or the things that our spouse complains about are usually the areas in which we could stand to experience more growth.

A TRUE STORY

Do you remember the story in the beginning of the book about the wife that was domestically challenged? For years the husband had complained. He had wanted a wife who would be a stay-at-home mom. She ended up having a passion for working. Instead he became Mr. Mom. While he didn't mind cooking, he felt a bit emasculated and taken advantage of. In turn, he was so overwhelmed at home that he did not get his act together as a breadwinner. The wife, on the other hand, complained about his lack of motivation to grow his business and his general low self-esteem.

The things they disliked about each other were the very things each one of them needed to grow. Growing up in a divorced home with a feminist mom who pushed work over motherhood, the wife realized that she had judgments about staying home. Even though her mother always had dinner on the table, she was never encouraged to learn more about how to take control of a kitchen and turn it into a pleasurable experience. She didn't even know how to boil water! Accepting more responsibilities at home allowed her to look at parts of herself that she never wanted to look at before. Not only did it help her become more balanced, it gave her husband what he so desperately needed in a wife. In turn, that freed up the husband to concentrate on what he needed to do: be productive and make a living. Knowing that domestic chores would be taken care of, he could shift his focus elsewhere, feel better about himself, and curb his wife's anxiety about his livelihood.

If this conflict were not resolved, you may have suggested that they were wrong for each other. He should have married someone more motherly. In fact, on one of their dates she said she wasn't the "mommy type." He was too in love to really believe it, and he was in for a rude awakening. Yet his need, and subsequent frustration, was what compelled her to grow. And perhaps she should have married a professional with a good job. Her need for him to work was just what he needed for his own self-esteem, to be the breadwinner.

Thus your marriage crisis is not proof that you ended up with the wrong person; rather, it shows that you made the right choice. The hopes of someone better are futile because Mr./Mrs. Right will serve as a vehicle for your personal growth. After the honeymoon ends, your spouse will surely push your buttons, but still, this is not proof that you ended up with the wrong person. Might as well give it your all and make it work the first time instead of breaking up a family, spending lots of money on attorneys, and suffering additional heartache.

Relationship Peace

What is more important than your marriage? If you don't have peace in your home then you will likely not have much peace of mind in anything you do. This reminds me of the following story:

There was once a Rabbi who stopped to rest at an inn. The innkeeper recognized who he was and asked for some private consultation time with the Rabbi. The innkeeper poured out his heart to the Rabbi. He complained about his wife and how she was so verbally abusive, giving him such a hard time about money and her overall nagging. While her husband was consulting with the Rabbi, the wife couldn't wait to put in her two cents. She couldn't wait to tell the Rabbi what was wrong with her husband. She piped up and told the Rabbi, "If there is no grinding in the mill, there is grinding in the home. If there is no business, there is no peace at home." The Rabbi replied, "On the contrary, if there is no grinding in the home, there is grinding in the mill. The best omen for business is peace in the home!"

Would you not give all the money and time in the world for peace?

Investing in your relationship

Again, this means redirecting yourself to your spouse and committing to success instead of looking elsewhere for something or someone better. If divorce is always an option lurking in the back of your mind, you will not be able to be fully present in your relationship. You lack the commitment to make your relationship work. That is why a couple can come to counseling and still not succeed. Their commitment can be seen in their attitude and their actions. My successful couples are the ones who come consistently on a weekly basis. In the past, I had a sliding-fee scale based on joint gross income. Every once in a while I had couples complain about the fee, and in certain cases I lowered it. I can tell you that every couple that had a fee reduction was unsuccessful. In my judgment, they were not truly invested in their relationship. This not only showed in their success rate but in their attendance. They would cancel sessions, skip weeks, etc... It got to the point where I would make a fee reduction contingent on committing to 12 weekly sessions. I knew from experience that if they did not make such a commitment, they would not get the results they were looking for. An investment is not always pleasant but it is the best assurance that you will put in the necessary effort. Otherwise, you risk a loss.

My wife recently went to hear a talk given by a parenting expert. He has a host of programs available on CD, all rather costly. He explained to the audience that he charges so much because he wants the purchase to "hurt a bit." How many of you had bought self-help books or programs, only to have them sitting and collecting dust on your shelf? Unless you have unlimited finances, if you invested $500 in a set of CDs, you'd make sure you use them.

In my experience, couples in crisis that want their marriage to succeed and are willing to invest in their relationship are almost always successful. This holds true even for extramarital affairs. It is astonishing how, even with such a breach in the relationship, it is possible to salvage a marriage by committing to making it work. The ones who lack that commitment are the ones who don't always make it.

The Freedom of Commitment

While you may be afraid of committing, once you decide to commit, you will actually feel much more relieved. A quote from a Starbucks cup: " The irony of commitment is that it's deeply liberating — in work, in play, in love. The acts frees you from the tyranny of your internal critic, from the fear that likes to dress itself up and parade around as rational hesitation. To commit is to remove your head as the barrier to your life."

It is often the case that indecision is what feels so uncomfortable and enslaving. Once we muster the courage to decide to commit, that stagnant energy can now move and propel you forward for thc good.

The following are three written exercises to help you make the decision and develop the attitude of commitment.

Exercise 1b - Committing to your marriage: Ask yourself the following questions

1) What is getting in the way of me committing to this relationship?

2) What is at risk for me to commit? What is so scary about it?

3) What will I gain if I do commit?

Exercise 1c - Memory Lane

This is a fun exercise that you can even do together with your spouse. Oftentimes we forget why we fell in love. When we begin to think back on that wonderful time of courtship, we begin to remember that there was a good reason why we got married. This can provide us hope for our relationship.

Close your eyes and take a trip down memory lane, remembering the time when you first fell in love. As you remember that time, please share or write down three qualities that you found in your spouse that helped you know "he/she is the one for me." When you are done, explain or write down why those qualities were so important to you at that time.

Exercise 1d - Relationship Dream

In order to commit to the future of your relationship, it is essential to have a vision of how you see your relationship and where you see it going. Although it may appear to be just a dream, it is useful for providing you perspective, instead of getting stuck in some of the current difficulties you may be encountering. Take all the time you need to dream about where you see your relationship going. Do you hope you will grow old together and feel forever like best friends?

Do you wish to hold respect for each other even when times are difficult? When you are ready, write down a list of sentences that embody your dream. Remember to write in the positive and in present tense. Instead of "we do not fight," write "we live peacefully together." Present tense is important because it brings your dream into the here and now, as if it is currently happening.

Summary of Action Step I

Lack of commitment is the number one reason for divorce. In order to save your marriage you need to commit. Commitment is a decision, an attitude and an action. It is a decision to be dedicated to your relationship and place it as a priority. From this decision, you develop the attitude that your marriage comes first. Finally, your actions manifest that attitude.

It is important to commit because marriage is not expendable. It is not something that you just throw away when it is no longer working. There are also many potential problems you will face by getting divorced. If you have children, you will be splitting their world in two and putting them at great risk for divorce as well as psychological problems. You will also be worse off financially as you will have to split whatever remaining assets you have with your ex. Finally, you won't find someone better. As you have a role in your marital woes, you will also bring that same person, yourself, with you into any new relationship. Until you get conscious about your own triggers, you will likely experience similar marital unhappiness in your new relationship.

Marriage is for the purpose of growth and healing and your conflict with your spouse is actually proof you chose the right partner. In fact, conflict is a growth opportunity, compelling you to become a more complete person by changing the very areas that annoy your spouse but are also the most difficult for you to alter. Commitment enables you to achieve your own potential through your relationship.

Finally, there is nothing more important than relationship peace. It brings about all blessings. That is why it is crucial to truly be invested in your relationship. If you never make the decision to commit and you allow divorce to lurk in the back of your head as a constant option, you are not giving your marriage a fair chance.

THE 5 STEP ACTION PLAN TO A HAPPY & HEALTHY MARRIAGE

THE MARRIAGE RESTORATION PROJECT

To purchase your copy of The Marriage Restoration Project full-length program, please visit us online at:

www.TheMarriageRestorationProject.com/program

With the divorce rate reaching epidemic proportions, *The Marriage Restoration Project* was created to uphold the institution of marriage and family by providing proven resources that make a difference. Much like a piece of priceless art can be restored after years of neglect, so too a marriage has the potential to be restored to its original connection. These five simple steps will help you get there.

Advanced praise for The Marriage Restoration Project:

"Any couple interested in restoring their marriage and sustaining it will be blessed if they follow the logical and clear steps and processes described by Rabbi Slatkin in the Marriage Restoration Project. The concepts are clear, the instructions are logical and the heart of the author are evident on every page."

    Harville Hendrix, Ph. D. co-author with Helen LaKelly Hunt of Making Marriage Simple: Ten Truths for Changing the Relationship You Have into the Relationship You Want.

"This program is such an amazing resource and I am honored to support your work. Thank you for all you are doing to make a difference".

    Kirk Martin Relationship Expert Founder of CelebrateCalm.com

 **Shlomo Slatkin** is a Licensed Clinical Professional Counselor, Certified Imago Relationship Therapist, and an ordained Rabbi. He works with couples to empower them to develop a conscious and connected relationship through learning communication skills and rediscovering love. Rabbi Slatkin also uses the Imago couple therapy model with individuals, families, and organizations.